T0063852

TOP **10**
DUBAI AND
ABU DHABI

Top 10 Dubai and Abu Dhabi Highlights

The Top 10 of Everything

CONTENTS

Dubai and Abu Dhabi Area by Area

Streetsmart

Within each Top 10 list in this book, no hierarchy of quality or popularity is implied. All 10 are, in the editor's opinion, of roughly equal merit.

Title page, front cover and spine *Dubai's stunning cityscape, seen from the waterfront on a cloudy evening*
Back cover, clockwise from top left *Dubai Souk's colourful stalls; traditional abra boat in Dubai Creek; Dubai skyline at sunset, viewed from the Arabian Desert; Burj Khalifa; aerial view of Dubai's coastline*

The rapid rate at which the world is changing is constantly keeping the DK Eyewitness team on our toes. While we've worked hard to ensure that this edition of Dubai and Abu Dhabi is accurate and up-to-date, we know that opening hours alter, standards shift, prices fluctuate, places close and new ones pop up in their stead. So, if you notice we've got something wrong or left something out, we want to hear about it. Please get in touch at **travelguides@dk.com**

Welcome to
Dubai and Abu Dhabi

Dubai and Abu Dhabi are two of the world's most exciting cities. Packed with soaring skyscrapers, chic shopping malls and luxury resorts, both offer a surfeit of indulgent pleasures and futuristic style. With DK Eyewitness Top 10 Dubai and Abu Dhabi, they're yours to explore.

Both these cities have rewritten the record books and established themselves as global icons with a plethora of mega-developments. Dubai's sail-shaped **Burj Al Arab Jumeirah** is one of the Middle East's most instantly recognizable landmarks, rivalled by the cloud-capped **Burj Khalifa**, the world's tallest building. In Abu Dhabi, the extravagant **Emirates Palace** and monumental **Sheikh Zayed Mosque** have set their own raft of records, with the **Louvre Abu Dhabi** adding lustre to the city's ever-growing array of attractions.

Although modern developments tend to hog the headlines, both cities, Dubai especially, have an older and more traditional side. The labyrinthine **souks** of Deira and the historic windtower houses of **Bur Dubai** are a joy to explore, while a ride on Dubai's breezy **creek** is the highlight of any visit. Outside the two cities, the desert landscape is spectacular, and is best appreciated with a drive across the dunes.

Whether you're coming for a weekend or a week, our Top 10 guide brings together the best of everything that the cities have to offer, from shopping for spices in the backstreets of **Deira** to the futuristic cityscapes of **Dubai Marina** and **Al Maryah Island**. The guide has useful tips throughout, from seeking out what's free to avoiding the crowds, plus nine easy-to-follow itineraries designed to tie together a clutch of sights in a short space of time. Add inspiring photography and detailed maps, and you've got the essential pocket-sized travel companion. **Enjoy the book, and enjoy Dubai and Abu Dhabi.**

Clockwise from top: **Dubai Marina at night, Burj Al Arab Jumeirah, traditional wooden** *dhow* in front of the Dubai Museum, water pool at Sheikh Zayed Mosque, Aladdin shoes in a Bur Dubai souk, desert hotel Anantara Qasr Al Sarab near the Liwa Oasis, aerial view of the Palm Jumeirah

Exploring Dubai and Abu Dhabi

Both Dubai and Abu Dhabi are very spread out, with miles of walkways around Dubai Marina, Palm Jumeirah and Downtown Dubai. Fortunately, Dubai's superb metro system also makes getting around easy, while in Abu Dhabi there are plenty of inexpensive taxis. Whether you have just a couple of days or more time to explore, here are some time-efficient ideas to help you make the most of your visit.

Burj Al Arab Jumeirah

Madinat Jumeirah

Dubai Marina

UMM SUQEIM

JUMEIRAH ISLANDS

Around Dubai

0 km 50
0 miles 50

Arabian Gulf

Sharjah

Area of main map

Desert Safari

Abu Dhabi

UNITED ARAB EMIRATES

OMAN

Al Ain

Two Days in Dubai

Day ❶
MORNING

Start the day with a visit to the **Dubai Museum** *(see pp14–15)*, and wander around the historic **Al Fahidi** district *(see pp18–19)*. Catch an *abra* across **Dubai Creek** *(see pp16–17)*, and then head over to Deira for exploring the colourful **Dubai souks** *(see pp26–7)*.

AFTERNOON

After lunch, head to the **Burj Al Arab Jumeirah** *(see pp24–5)* for afternoon tea. Then stroll over to the **Madinat Jumeirah** *(see p79)* at sunset.

Day ❷
MORNING

Begin with a visit to the soaring **Burj Khalifa**

(see pp12–13) for spectacular panoramic views over the city, and then browse the super-chic shops of the adjacent **Dubai Mall** *(see p73)*.

AFTERNOON

Head out into the sands for a **desert safari** *(see p32)*, starting with a spot of dune bashing. Round off the day with an evening of henna painting, belly dancing and other traditional activities.

Seven Days in Dubai and Abu Dhabi

Day ❶

Start by visiting the **Dubai Museum** *(see pp14–15)* and then explore the historic **Al Fahidi** *(see pp18–19)* and **Shindagha** districts *(see p16)*. Towards mid-afternoon head out of the city on a **desert safari** *(see p32)*.

Dubai Mall, the world's largest shopping mall, is packed with stores, food outlets and attractions.

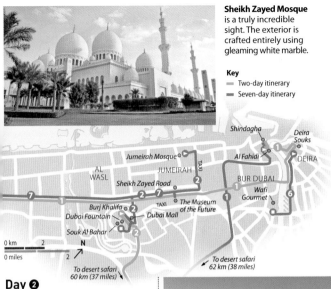

Sheikh Zayed Mosque is a truly incredible sight. The exterior is crafted entirely using gleaming white marble.

Key
— Two-day itinerary
— Seven-day itinerary

Day ❷
Visit the beautiful **Jumeirah Mosque** *(see pp20–21)*, then take a taxi or metro via **Sheikh Zayed Road** *(see pp70–73)* to the **Dubai Mall** *(see p73)* and **Souk Al Bahar** *(see p72)*. Watch the dazzling **Dubai Fountain** *(see p71)* from the bridge connecting Souk Al Bahar and Dubai Mall. At sunset, head up the **Burj Khalifa** *(see pp12–13)* for stunning views.

Day ❸
Take a day trip to explore either the excellent museums and traditional buildings of **Sharjah** *(see p54)* or the marvellous mud-brick forts and oases of idyllic **Al Ain** *(see p54)*.

Day ❹
Head to **Abu Dhabi** *(see pp90–101)* to spend a day exploring the Downtown area and the wonderful **Corniche** *(see pp90–93)*. Book in advance for afternoon tea or dinner at opulent **Emirates Palace** *(see pp30–31)*.

Day ❺
Visit the monumental **Sheikh Zayed Mosque** *(see pp28–9)*, then head down to the **Louvre Abu Dhabi** *(see p97)* before returning to Dubai.

A desert safari is a popular and thrilling way of seeing the desert.

Day ❻
Explore the labyrinthine souks in Deira *(see pp26–7)*. Then head down to the Egyptian-themed **Wafi Gourmet** *(see p68)* for drinks and a well-deserved rest.

Day ❼
Spend the morning exploring the varied sights around **Dubai Marina** *(see p83)*. Next, head to the iconic **Burj Al Arab Jumeirah** *(see pp24–5)* for afternoon tea. Later in the evening, explore the stunning **Madinat Jumeirah** *(see p79)*.

Top 10 Dubai and Abu Dhabi Highlights

The entrance to Sheikh Zayed Mosque at dusk, Abu Dhabi

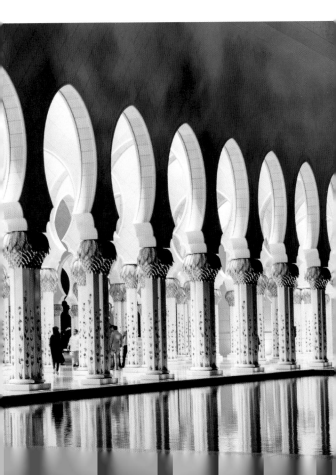

🔟 Dubai and Abu Dhabi Highlights

The cities of Dubai and Abu Dhabi offer the best of East and West – Arab culture, Bedouin heritage and Islamic architecture, plus sophisticated shopping, dining and hotels. Dubai is set around its creek and skirted with white-sand beaches, while Abu Dhabi is located on a fine corniche.

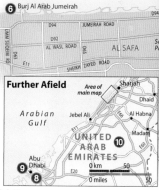

Dubai Museum ②

The Dubai Museum is housed inside an 18th-century fort and boats fascinating displays that provide great insight into the city *(see pp14–15)*.

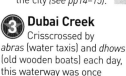

① Burj Khalifa

The world's tallest building and the jewel in the crown of modern Dubai *(see pp12–13)*.

③ Dubai Creek

Crisscrossed by *abras* (water taxis) and *dhows* (old wooden boats) each day, this waterway was once Dubai's lifeblood *(see pp16–17)*.

⑥ Burj Al Arab Jumeirah

④ Al Fahidi

The gypsum and coral courtyard houses in this quarter (previously known as Bastakiya) were built by Persian merchants who settled here in the 20th century *(see pp18–19)*.

Jumeirah Mosque ⑤

Not only is this Dubai's most beautiful mosque, it is also one of the few mosques open to non-Muslims. A guided visit to learn about Islamic culture is a must *(see pp20–21)*.

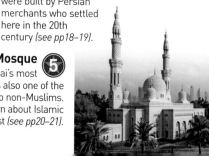

Burj Al Arab Jumeirah 6

This iconic "seven-star" hotel has long been the defining symbol of Dubai and is still a recognizable landmark, rising high above the coast *(see pp24–5)*.

7 Dubai Souks

Bargain for gold, perfume, spices and textiles, or simply take in the heady atmosphere of Dubai's souks *(see pp26–7)*.

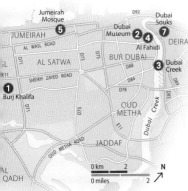

8 Sheikh Zayed Mosque

This vast, snowy-white mosque is topped with myriad domes and minarets. The immense prayer hall is a real highlight *(see pp28–9)*.

9 Emirates Palace

The jaw-dropping display of gold lining the walls and Swarovski crystals dripping from the chandeliers at Abu Dhabi's Emirates Palace hotel make for an impressive sight *(see pp30–31)*.

Desert Escapes 10

A visit to the United Arab Emirates (UAE) is incomplete without a desert experience. Stay in an enchanting resort or take a fun desert safari *(see pp32–3)*.

🔟 ⭐ Burj Khalifa and Around

Opened in 2010, the Burj Khalifa is by far the tallest building on the planet (828 m/2,716 ft). Its needle-thin outline soars high above Dubai and is visible from almost 100 km (62 miles) away. The Burj Khalifa was planned as the centrepiece of the multi-billion-dollar Downtown Dubai development, but only when prompted by Dubai ruler Sheikh Mohammed did architects consider making it the tallest building in the world and a true symbol of Dubai's towering ambitions.

1 Armani Hotel Dubai

Occupying several of Burj Khalifa's lower floors is the world's first Armani Hotel Dubai, showcasing the Italian designer's chic minimalist style **(below)**. The hotel has trendy bars and restaurants, which are open to non-guests.

Burj Khalifa and its surroundings lit up at night

2 The Exhibition

Interesting displays scattered around the entrance foyer and en route to the observation decks chart the history of the construction of the Burj, commemorating some of the leading figures involved. A display of fascinating photos also show the tower when it was under construction.

3 Burj Khalifa

The two observation decks offer incredible views for miles around. The views straight down over Downtown Dubai are particularly stunning, with buildings reduced to the size of neat models, clustered around the intense-blue outline of the Burj Khalifa Lake.

NEED TO KNOW

MAP C6

Burj Khalifa: 1 Sheikh Mohammed bin Rashid Boulevard, Downtown Dubai; 04 888 8888; open 8:30am–10pm daily; adm adults AED 125–500, children AED 95–500; www.burjkhalifa.ae

Armani Hotel Dubai: 04 888 3888; www. armanihotels.com

The Address Downtown: 04 436 8888; www.the address.com

■ The two observation decks are on floors 125 and 148. Entrance is via the Dubai Mall *(see p73)*.

Tickets are cheaper for floor 124 if pre-booked online, but prices rise for sunset. Combination tickets for floors 124 and 148 must be pre-booked and also cost more at sunset.

■ Visit the site in the evening to watch the Dubai Fountain *(see p71)* choreographed to music.

Souk Al Bahar and Old Town ④

On the southern side of Burj Khalifa Lake is Souk Al Bahar *(see p72)*. This area mark a significant change in architectural tone from other nearby buildings **(right)** with low-rise, sand-coloured Arabian-style design.

Dubai Opera ⑥

Nestled next to Burj Khalifa, this performing arts centre is Dubai's top creative destination, hosting among the finest theatre performances, opera, concerts, ballet and exhibitions from around the globe.

Sheikh Zayed Road ⑦

Looking north from the building's observation deck, the view is dominated by Sheikh Zayed Road's long line of spiky skyscrapers, although the height of the Burj means that even the tallest is reduced to relative insignificance.

At.Mosphere ⑩

The world's highest bar and restaurant *(see p75)* are on Burj Khalifa's 122nd floor. Fine dining and cocktails in the clouds are the theme here.

The Address Downtown ⑤

Dominating the view to the southeast of the Burj Khalifa is the huge 72-storey Address Downtown hotel **(below)**, with its unusual semi-circular summit. Head to Neos cocktail bar on the 63rd floor for a different perspective of Downtown Dubai.

Jumeirah ⑧

Looking west from Burj Khalifa, the sea is relatively close at hand, with glimpses of the beach and views over the suburb of Jumeirah *(see pp76–81)*, with its endless sprawl of low, milky-white villas.

Burj Al Arab Jumeirah and Beyond ⑨

At the far southern end of Jumeirah rises the outline of the Burj Al Arab hotel *(see pp24–5)*. Although it's over 10 km (6 miles) away, the hotel's size means that it's clearly visible. Beyond, you can make out the outline of the Palm Jumeirah and the skyscrapers of the marina.

TOP 10 TOWER FACTS

1 It has more floors (163) than any other building.

2 The world's highest mosque (158th floor) can be found here.

3 Lifts reach speeds of 10 meters per second.

4 More than 12,000 people worked on its construction.

5 A World War II airplane engine was used to test the wind resistance.

6 It takes three months to clean the windows.

7 The total aluminum used is equal to five Airbus 380s.

8 The spire is made from over 4,000 tons of steel.

9 Pressurized refuges on every 25th floor provide safety from fires.

10 It is named after the second President of UAE, Sheikh Khalifa bin Zayed Al Nahyan.

🔟⭐ Dubai Museum

This cleverly planned museum makes a great starting point for a tour of Dubai. It gives an insight into traditions past and present, and offers a vivid picture of how Dubai has crammed into five decades what most cities achieve in several centuries. Located in the historic creekside Al Fahidi district *(see pp18–19)*, the museum is set within and beneath one of the city's oldest buildings, Al Fahidi Fort. It traces the city's meteoric development from a small desert settlement to the centre of the Arab world for commerce, finance and tourism.

① Archaeological Finds

Interesting artifacts from excavations of graves that date back to 3,000 BCE are on display, including fine copper and alabaster objects and a selection of pottery **(above)**.

② Desert at Night Exhibitions

Learn how animals that live in the Arabian desert have adapted to cope with the lack of water, extreme temperatures and shortage of food.

③ Multimedia Presentation

An interesting 10-minute film presentation with archive footage explains the development of modern Dubai from 1960 onward. The film takes you through a decade-by-decade pictorial tour of Dubai's transformation over the past 50 years.

④ Old Dubai Souk Dioramas

Holographic technology combined with waxwork figures **(below)**, smells, sounds and archive footage help transport visitors back in time to the creekside souks of half a century ago.

⑤ Al Fahidi Fort

Constructed in 1787, this fort, with its magnificent watchtower, was built to defend the Emiratis against invasion. Renovated in 1971, it now serves as a city museum.

BEDOUIN CULTURE

Bedu, the Arabic word from which the name Bedouin is derived, means "inhabitant of the desert". Bedouins would move from oasis to oasis by camel and engage in small-scale agriculture. The hardships of the desert have imbued Bedouin culture with a strong honour code and a famous hospitality.

Courtyard Barasti and Windtower House ⑥

The courtyard in the Al Fahidi Fort *(see p19)* houses a *barasti* (date-palm frond) house **(right)** and windtower cooling system, which were both commonly seen in the region as recently as the 1950s.

Floorplan of Dubai Museum

Key to Floorplan
- Ground Floor
- Basement

NEED TO KNOW

MAP K2 ■ Al Fahidi Fort, Al Fahidi St ■ 800 33222 ■ www.dubai tourism.ae

Closed for renovation

■ The Dubai Museum located within the Al Fahidi Fort is closed for renovation until further notice but views of the magnificent historical monument can be enjoyed from the outside. Call ahead or check the website before visiting.

⑦ Wooden Dhow

A traditional Arab *dhow* **(above)** is on show at the exit. For celestial navigation, sailors used the *kamal*, a device that determines latitude using the angle of the Pole Star above the horizon.

⑩ Underwater Pearl-Diving Exhibition

This interesting gallery explains the techniques used by pearl divers who wore nose clips and weights to descend to impossible depths.

⑧ Islamic School Dioramas

Young Emiratis recite the lines of the Koran under the watchful eye of their tutor in this reconstruction of a 1950s school.

Bedouin Traditions Display ⑨

A gallery displays the costumes, jewellery, weapons **(right)** and tools of the Bedouin people.

TOP 10 ⭐ Dubai Creek

Dubai Creek, fed by the waters of the Arabian Gulf, is the lifeblood of old and new Dubai. The contrast of traditional wooden *dhows* at the wharfage against stunning modern architecture, such as the glass dome-fronted Emirates National Bank of Dubai and the giant ball-topped Etisalat building, is striking. The two sides of the creek are Deira (north) and Bur Dubai (south) and a walk along either is an ideal way to discover this multi-faceted city. Getting across the creek is easy: the nearest bridges for cars are Maktoum Bridge and Garhoud Bridge but the cheapest crossing is by *abra*.

② Bur Dubai Waterfront

The Diwan and historic architecture of "Old Dubai" are best enjoyed from the Deira side of the creek: here you can see windtowers, minarets and the domes of the Grand Mosque.

③ Shindagha Heritage

In the Shindagha area near the mouth of the Dubai Creek, you will find the Al Shindagha Museum *(see p66)*, which includes a group of heritage houses and an exhibition charting the development of the city since its birth.

① The Diwan

With its modern white windtowers and imposing wrought-iron gates *(see p65)*, the Diwan **(above)**, or Ruler's Office, is an impressive and important building.

NEED TO KNOW
MAP K1–K4

Creek Park: 04 800 900; open 8am–11pm Sun–Wed, 8am–11:30pm Thu–Sat; adm AED 5; www.dm.gov.ae

Abra Crossing:
Route 1: 5am–midnight, Route 2: 24 hours; AED 1 each way

Bateaux Dubai:
04 814 5553/04 336 6768; boarding is between 7:15 and 7:45pm, departs 8pm

daily; reservations. bateauxdubai.com

Dhow Cruise Tour: 056 620 9095; www.dhowcruisetour.com

Al Seef: open 10am–10pm daily (until midnight Thu & Fri)

■ By night, admire the illuminated *dhows* as they glide along the creek.

■ For refreshment, stop for a cooling fresh juice at the Textile Souk *(see p27)*.

Map of Dubai Creek

④ Creek Park

A wonderful expanse of parkland, Creek Park stretches along the water's edge. Walk its length and enjoy the vistas or enjoy a round of mini golf or go-karting.

7 Emirates National Bank of Dubai

One of Dubai's very first Modernist high-rises (see p59) is still one of its most memorable (**left**). The curved façade (inspired by the shape of a *dhow's* hull) reflects the water below.

9 Creek Cruises

Tour operators offer romantic dinner cruises along the creek each evening aboard traditional wooden *dhows*, often accompanied by belly-dancing and live Arabian music. The sleek Bateaux Dubai offers a more modern and luxurious option.

5 Dubai Creek Golf Club

The Dubai Creek Golf Club building (**above**) is one of the city's most unusual Modernist landmarks (see p60), with glass-fronted façades nestled beneath three spiky white "sails".

6 Dhow Wharfage

Stroll beside the creek along Baniyas Road, where colourfully painted wooden *dhows* (**below**) are moored and boats arrive from Iran, Oman and the rest of the UAE.

8 Abra Trips

Dubai's open-sided, flat-bottomed water taxis are called *abras*. These provide a breezy way to travel the creek, and carry 40,000 people per day. Hop in with other passengers and enjoy the views.

HISTORY OF DUBAI CREEK

Once a tiny fishing settlement sprawled around the mouth of the creek, *Dibei*, as it was known in the 16th century, owes its existence to the 14-km (9-mile) Dubai Creek, which led into a natural harbour and established itself as a flourishing hub for entrepôt trade.

10 Al Seef

Sprawled along the Dubai Creek shoreline, Al Seef was once home to pearl divers, weavers and traders. It now offers a charming blend of culture and heritage, with shops, cafés and restaurants tucked along the marina.

TOP 10 ★ Al Fahidi

The beautifully restored old Al Fahidi quarter (previously known by its old name of Bastakiya) gives a picturesque glimpse into the city's past, in sharp contrast to the futuristic architecture found elsewhere. As you wander the maze of shady streets and alleys, traditional windtower houses with elegant courtyards can be seen in sand, stone, coral and gypsum. The buildings have been restored to their original state, with Arabesque windows, decorative gypsum panels and screens. This area is home to art galleries, museums and cafés.

1 Traditional Architecture

The need to remain cool prompted the vernacular style of the windtower courtyard houses. Thick walls and narrow windows with intricate Arabesque designs are featured.

2 Majlis Gallery

Named after the Arabic word for a meeting place, Majlis (see p38) is a bijou art gallery built around a beautifully converted whitewashed Arabic house with a central garden. It houses the works of both local Emirati as well as expat artists, and features original pottery, ceramics, crafts and jewellery.

3 Coins Museum

The Coins Museum showcases Arabian money **(left)** through the ages. Almost 500 coins are on display from Ummayad to Ottoman times, with touchscreens providing fascinating historical information.

4 Sheikh Mohammed Centre for Cultural Understanding

This pioneering centre aims to give visitors and expats a deeper understanding of Emirati culture. A number of activities are available, including walking tours of Al Fahidi (see p55) and regular "cultural" breakfasts and lunches.

5 Coffee Museum

This museum (see p67) reveals the history of the region's favourite drink. Exhibits **(above)** include old-fashioned grinders, coffee pots and antique tins. Make sure to try the Arabian-style coffee.

6 Old City Wall

Restoration work of the original 200-year-old city wall **(left)** has drawn attention to the history of this section of the city as a crucial defensive zone.

7 Bastakiah Nights Restaurant

With its courtyard setting, this restaurant offers an Arabian atmosphere best experienced after dusk. The restored building **(left)** has been traditionally furnished, with Arabian and Emirati food served inside or on the rooftop.

NEED TO KNOW

MAP K2

Coins Museum: 800 33222; open 8–11:30am Fri

Sheikh Mohammed Centre for Cultural Understanding: 04 353 6666; open 8am–5pm Sun–Thu, 9am–1pm Sat; www.cultures.ae

Coffee Museum: 04 353 8777; open 9am–5pm Sat–Thu; www.coffee museum.ae

Bastakiah Nights Restaurant: 04 353 7772; open 11am–10pm daily

■ Visit Al Fahidi late in the day when the golden light and long shadows add to the atmosphere.

■ For lunch, the Arabian Tea House Café *(see p69)* offers a great Lebanese and Middle-Eastern menu for healthy light meals and snacks, fresh soup and salad.

10 Arabian Tea House Café

Located in a traditional courtyard of an Al Fahidi house, this café *(see p69)* is a great spot to sit amid flowering bougainvillea and enjoy lunch.

WINDTOWERS

The most distinctive architectural element of Arabian houses in the early 20th century, windtowers *(barjeel)* were designed to create natural ventilation. With four open sides, each of which was hollowed into a concave v-shape, windtowers deflected the air down, cooling the rooms below. Water was thrown on the floor beneath the tower to cool the house further.

8 Al Fahidi Fort

Built in 1787, this fort is the oldest building in Dubai. Its original walls were built from coral and shell rubble. It now houses the Dubai Museum *(see pp14–15)*, which is closed for renovation.

9 XVA Gallery, Café and Hotel

Contemporary art is on display in galleries off the courtyard of this restored traditional house **(right)**. It is also home to a café and hotel *(see p38)*.

TOP 10 ★ Jumeirah Mosque

Dubai's culture is rooted in Islam, a fact that touches all aspects of everyday life. Virtually every neighbourhood has its own mosque, but undoubtedly the jewel in the crown is the Jumeirah Mosque. This fine example of modern Islamic architecture was built in 1979. It is a dramatic sight set against blue skies and is especially breathtaking at night, when it is lit up and its artistry is thrown into relief. Built of smooth white stone, the mosque, with its elaborately decorated twin minarets and majestic dome, is a city landmark and an important place of worship.

1 A Precious Gift

The mesmerizingly beautiful Jumeirah Mosque was a gift to the people of Dubai from its late ruler Sheikh Rashid bin Saeed Al Maktoum, father of the current ruler, Sheikh Mohammed bin Rashid Al Maktoum.

3 Mosque Architecture

With its vast central dome, this mosque **(right)** is inspired by the Anatolian style. The exterior is decorated in geometric relief over the stonework.

2 Ramadan

During the holy month of Ramadan (the ninth month of the Islamic calendar), Muslims abstain from food, drink and other physical needs from dawn until sunset. This is a time for purification and for focussing on Allah.

NEED TO KNOW

MAP E4 ■ Al Jumeirah Rd, Jumeirah ■ 04 353 6666

Mosque Tours: 10am Sat–Thu, visitors are required to assemble by the entrance 10 minutes in advance (no booking required); adm AED 35, under 12s free

■ Close to the mosque, the Lime Tree Café *(see p81)* serves sandwiches, cakes and coffee.

■ La Mer beach is also located close by, and has several restaurants and sheesha spots.

■ Tours are intended to help visitors gain a real understanding of Islam. Photography is permitted inside the mosque.

■ Each tour lasts about 75 minutes. Admission includes water, dates, Arabic coffee, tea and traditional pastries.

5 Prayers

The *adhan* (call to prayer) rings out from the minarets five times a day – all able Muslims must supplicate themselves **(above)** to Allah by praying on a *musalla* (traditional mat).

6 Five Pillars of Islam

The "Five Pillars of Islam" are: *Shahadah*, the belief in the oneness of God; *Salat*, the five daily prayers; *Zakat*, alms-giving; *Siyam*, self-purification and *Hajj*, the pilgrimage to Mecca.

CALL TO PRAYER

Wherever you are in Dubai, you are likely to be within earshot of a mosque and to hear the daily calls to prayer *"Allahu akbar"* (God is great). Today, the modern-day call is transmitted through loudspeakers; in the past the muezzin made the call himself.

9 Mihrab

The *mihrab* **(below)** is the niche in the wall of this and every mosque. Its purpose is to indicate the *qibla*, the direction a Muslim should face when praying. This *mihrab* gives the impression of a door or a passage to Mecca.

4 "Open Doors, Open Minds" Guided Tours

Jumeirah Mosque is one of only a couple of mosques in Dubai open to the public. The "Open Doors, Open Minds" interactive guided mosque tour is run by the Sheikh Mohammed Centre for Cultural Understanding *(see p18)*. It offers a great opportunity to gain insight into the Islamic faith.

7 Minarets

Two minarets crown this mosque. The height of the tallest minaret – the highest point of the "House of Allah" – is determined by how far the call to prayer should be heard.

8 Minbar

The *minbar* is the pulpit from which the *Imam* (leader of prayer) stands to deliver the *khutba* (Friday sermon).

10 Mosque Etiquette

Dubai may be very cosmopolitan, but in keeping with mosque etiquette, you must dress conservatively to enter. No shorts or sleeveless tops for either gender; women must wear a headscarf. Remove your shoes before entering.

Following pages The beautiful interior of the Sheikh Zayed Mosque

TOP 10 ⭐ Burj Al Arab Jumeirah

So recognizable that it instantly became an international symbol for modern Dubai, the Burj Al Arab Jumeirah (meaning "Arabian tower"), completed in 1999, is an exclusive all-suite hotel. With its helipad on the 28th floor and a restaurant seemingly suspended in mid-air, it is a place of sheer decadence. At a soaring 321 m (1,053 ft), it also takes the trophy for being the world's tallest all-suite hotel. Set on its own artificial island against the backdrop of the turquoise waters of the Gulf, it is dazzling white by day and rainbow-coloured by night, when its façade is used as a canvas for spectacular light displays.

NEED TO KNOW

MAP C1 ■ Jumeirah Rd, Dubai ■ 04 301 7777 ■ www.jumeirah.com

L'Olivo at Al Mahara: open 6:30–10pm

Skyview Bar: open noon–2am

■ In order to enter the hotel, you must have a reservation for a meal, cocktails or afternoon tea. To do this, call the hotel at 04 301 7600 or email BAArestaurants@ jumeirah.com. The most affordable options here are drinks at Gold On 27 and at Scape Restaurant & Bar, or food at Bab Al Yam restaurant.

■ The dress code at Gold On 27 and Scape Restaurant & Bar is "stylish chic", and smart casual dress is required at Bab Al Yam.

1 Talise Spa
Perched on the 18th floor, Talise Spa is an idyllic retreat with soothing ocean views. The beautiful decor is reminiscent of baths used by ancient Middle Eastern civilizations. There are panoramic views from the infinity pools.

2 The Exterior
The shore-facing façade of the Burj is covered by what looks like stretched translucent fabric. This is Teflon-coated woven glass fibre. It is the first time such technology has been used in this way in any building worldwide.

3 Skyview Bar
With its sky-high location, this rooftop bar offers the most amazing vistas of the shimmering coastline. The bar – a must for cocktails at sunset – is reached by an express panoramic lift.

4 Lobby
The lobby of the Burj is an airy space of marbles, mosaics and hand-crafted carpets in swirling patterns. There is an impressive multi-hued dancing fountain.

5 The Atrium
The Atrium's vast gold-leaf-covered columns and many layers of floors rising up from the lobby (above) create a dizzying sensation.

🔟 The Helipad

Jutting out of the Burj's summit, the building's iconic helipad **(below)** has featured in numerous commercials. It also serves as a unique wedding venue, and once hosted a game of tennis between Andre Agassi and Roger Federer.

6️⃣ Suites

The 202 amazing duplex suites **(above)** are equipped with the latest remote technology, plus in-suite check-in and personal butler service. The hotel's Royal Suite has been converted into a museum offering inside tours of the Burj Al Arab.

9️⃣ Architectural Inspiration

The billowing sail of the Arabian *dhow* was the inspiration for this contemporary creation **(below)**. Access for guests is by helicopter or car via the causeway. Rolls-Royce transfers are available.

7️⃣ Fish Tanks

The lobby features a pair of enormous tropical aquariums. They are so large that members of the hotel staff have to put on diving suits in order to clean them out.

8️⃣ L'Olivo at Al Mahara

At the base of the tower, this lavish, intimate seafood restaurant is helmed by chef Andrea Migliaccio of the Michelin-stared Ristorante L'Olivo in Capri.

THE CONSTRUCTION

The Burj Al Arab Jumeirah is said to be one of the most expensive buildings ever constructed. An estimated $2 billion was spent on it, though the full cost has never been revealed. Built on its own artificial island (which took three years to reclaim), the Burj al Arab Jumeirah rises to a height of 321 m (1,053 ft); it was the world's tallest hotel until 2007. Inside, the building's dazzling decor incorporates over 30 types of marble and 8,000 sq m (86,111 sq ft) of shimmering 22-carat gold leaf ornamentation.

TOP 10 ⭐ Dubai Souks

Shopping in Dubai is a shopaholic's dream, with almost nothing that cannot be bought here, but away from the air-conditioned marble-floored shopping malls is another experience: the souks. Many of these, such as the gold, textile and spice souks clustered beside the creek, date back to Dubai's beginnings as a palm-fringed trading port. Exploring their warren-like alleyways is a delight. Generally, each type of stall, be it spices, crafts, perfumes or clothing, are located close together, making it easy to spot a good deal. Bring cash and keep in mind that bargaining is expected.

1 Naif Souk, Deira

A kitsch faux desert fort houses this traditional-style souk selling everything from leather goods to electronics. It's popular with local women for its selection of abaya cloaks.

3 Grand Souk Deira

This souk feels more Indian than Arabic, with a medley of merchandise offered: colourful textiles, spices, kitchenware, clothes and henna.

2 Gold Souk

This souk gleams with gold **(below)**, silver and gems. Prices are competitive; dealers come in from around the globe and strict regulations are followed.

VISIT TO A TAILOR'S

Dubai is a wonderful place for tailoring, with an incredible array of textiles being widely available. Various tailors' shops can be found around the Textile Souk, but also elsewhere in Satwa and Bur Dubai. Most tailors will make an exact replica from the original item or a photograph, or you can select from their range of pattern books.

Map of the Dubai Souks

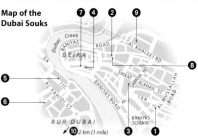

4 Deira Grand Souk

Sprawling behind the Spice Souk, Deira's Al Souk Al Kabeer ("Big Souk") boasts hundreds of shoe shops clad in coral-stone façades. The cute little Al Arsa Courtyard at the back is especially pretty.

7 Deira Spice Souk

This tiny souk is a real sensory delight. You can purchase aromatic frankincense and myrrh (with charcoal burners for them), plus a wide array of flavourful dried fruits and spices **(left)** such as cloves, cardamom and cinnamon. Iranian saffron is also particularly good value.

NEED TO KNOW

Open 10am–10pm (some souks shut at 1:30pm while shopkeepers attend the afternoon prayers)
■ www.dubaitourism.ae

■ Bargaining is expected. Start at half the initial price and haggle until you reach a compromise.

■ Tax-free prices in Dubai make luxury items such as perfume and electronic goods highly affordable.

■ Around the Bur Dubai souks are good-value Indian restaurants.

9 Waterfront Market

Great piles of colourful fruit and vegetables (especially dates), huge hunks of meat and heaps of ocean-fresh hammour and shark are just some of the foodstuffs on offer at this bustling souk.

10 Karama Souk

This souk offers "copy" items, especially watches and handbags. The quality of much of the products **(below)**, despite being fake, is very good.

5 Bur Dubai Textile Souk

Beautifully restored, this creekside souk **(above)** is covered by an arched pergola. It makes for an atmospheric walkway lined with little stalls selling reels of coloured cloth.

6 Bur Dubai Meena Bazaar

Be warned, a visit here may necessitate a trip to a tailor. Wonderful fabrics from all over the world, in every colour and texture imaginable (silks, satins, brocades, linens and more), are laid out before you.

8 Deira Perfume Souk

Fascinating shops sell heavy scents like jasmine, oudh, amber and rose, and will also mix individual "signature scents". Traditional Arabian *attars* are for sale alongside well-known Western brands.

TOP 10 ⭐ Sheikh Zayed Mosque

Standing guard over the city, the monumental Sheikh Zayed Mosque is the largest in the UAE. It has room for 50,000 worshippers and attracts vast crowds during festivals such as Eid. Built between 1996 and 2007, the mosque was the brainchild of the late president of the UAE, Sheikh Zayed bin Sultan Al Nahyan. Vast quantities of marble, gold, semiprecious stones and crystals were used in the construction, while the Pan-Islamic design unites styles including Persian, Mughal and Moorish.

① The Exterior

The outline of the mosque, with its four great minarets, dominates all approaches to the city. Covered in snowy-white Sivec marble from Macedonia, the building is topped with 82 domes.

④ The Prayer Hall Carpet

The floor of the main prayer hall is covered in a single vast carpet, the largest in the world. Made in Iran, the carpet is over 5,000 sq m (53,819 sq ft) in size, weighs around 35 tonnes and contains nearly 2.26 million knots.

⑤ The Prayer Hall Chandelier

Hanging magnificently above the centre of the prayer hall is the largest of the mosque's seven huge chandeliers. Produced in Germany, this is the third biggest chandelier in the world – measuring some 10 m (33 ft) wide and 15 m (49 ft) high. It was made using over a million Swarovski crystals.

⑥ The Minarets

Four minarets stand at each corner of the courtyard, rising some 107 m (351 ft) high. The design of the minarets fuses Mamluk, Ottoman and Fatimid styles from Turkey and Egypt, symbolizing the diverse traditions of Islamic architecture around the world.

② The Prayer Hall

The cavernous main prayer hall (above) is an extravagant showpiece of decoration and design, supported by 96 marble-clad columns inlaid with mother of pearl. The hall is capable of holding over 7,000 worshippers.

③ The Entrance

Entrance to the mosque is via a grand white arcade (right), with lines of gold-topped pillars to either side. The entrance is fronted by long pools of water.

8 The Qibla

The prayer hall's *qibla* wall (indicating the direction in which Mecca lies) has a golden alcove set into the wall **(left)** surrounded by the 99 names of Allah written in traditional Kufic calligraphy.

SHEIKH ZAYED

Former ruler of Abu Dhabi and "Father of the UAE", Sheikh Zayed bin Sultan Al Nahyan (1918–2004) became leader of Abu Dhabi in 1966, replacing his elder brother following a peaceful deposition. He initiated a programme that launched the emirate's transformation from an Arabian backwater to a global destination. In 1971, he also became the first president of the UAE. Famed for his generosity, Zayed remains a revered figure throughout the country.

10 The Minbar

Sitting alongside the *qibla* alcove is the small *minbar* or pulpit, **(below)** from which sermons are delivered during Friday Prayers.

7 The Courtyard

The vast courtyard **(above)** has space for 30,000 worshippers and is dazzlingly bright during the day. The floral mosaic, picked out in marble on the floor, is said to be the largest in the world.

9 Tomb of Sheikh Zayed

Outside the mosque is the tomb of Abu Dhabi's former ruler, Sheikh Zayed bin Sultan Al Nahyan. The tomb is as understated as the rest of the mosque is ornate.

NEED TO KNOW

MAP V3 ■ Khaleej al Arabi and Sheikh Rashid bin Saeed streets ■ 02 419 1919 ■ www.szgmc.gov.ae/en

Open 9am–10pm Sat–Thu, 4:30–10pm Fri

Free guided tours: 10am, 11am & 5pm Sat–Thu (also 2pm & 7pm Sat), 5pm & 7pm Fri

■ Visitors must remove shoes and cover arms and legs. Women are asked to wear a robe and headscarf (provided free).

■ The 5pm Sunset Tour is a nice time of day to see the mosque, and the building also looks spectacular after dark, with a unique lighting system designed to reflect the phases of the moon.

■ For refreshment head to the nearby Souk Qaryat al Beri (*see p97*), with its many cafés and restaurants.

🔟 ⭐ Emirates Palace

The stupendous Emirates Palace hotel dominates Downtown Abu Dhabi's southwestern side. Opened in 2005 to rival Dubai's Burj Al Arab Jumeirah, the hotel cost a reputed $3 billion and is built on the grandest of scales, stretching for well over a kilometre along its own exclusive beach. The hotel's majestic red-sandstone exterior, topped with rippling domes and surrounded by gushing fountains, is guaranteed to impress. Even more spectacular, however, is the lavish interior, a dazzling, shimmering vision of marble, gold leaf and opulent decorative features.

NEED TO KNOW

MAP N1 ■ West Corniche Rd, Abu Dhabi ■ 02 690 8888 ■ www.emiratespalace.com

■ Officially you need an advance reservation to get into the hotel. However, the lobby is open to the public. Email guestrelation@emiratespalace.ae for reservations.

■ Emirates Palace Spa offers an array of excellent spa escapes, such as the 24 Carat Gold Radiance Facial.

■ Two of Abu Dhabi's Michelin-starred restaurants are located at the hotel: Hakkasan *(02 690 7739; open 6–11:30pm)* and Talea by Antonio Guida *(02 690 8888; open 12:30–3pm & 6:30–11pm).* Reservations essential.

① Swarovski Crystal Chandeliers

Numerous chandeliers crafted using Swarovski crystals adorn the interior of the Palace. These are used like light bulbs and appear to be sparkling in every single room.

② Triumphant Arch

Before entering Emirates Palace you'll be dazzled by a majestic pink Triumphant Arch gate with a dome on top and a long and grand driveway **(left)**. The gate is usually closed but opened for royalty and dignitaries on special occasions.

③ Majlis with Arabian Horse Mural

The most impressive of the many plush public spaces here is the *majlis* (meeting area). It has a blue ceiling with frescoes and a magnificent mural of Arab stallions.

④ Emirates Palace Auditorium

This is a sophisticated venue that hosts Russian ballet, Arabic orchestra concerts and musical shows. It has incredible audio-visual technology, ornate interiors, and the capacity to accommodate 1,100 guests.

Palace Suites (5)

Emirates Palace has 302 plush rooms and 92 sumptuously decorated Khaleej and Palace Suites. On the fifth floor is a reception for kings and heads of state and on the eighth are suites designed especially for the Gulf Rulers. The Saudi suite **(right)** even has its own barbershop.

(9) Palace Gardens and Fountains

The palace's exterior **(left)** adopts traditional Arabian architectural elements and is painted to reflect the variations in colour of the Arabian sands. It is beautifully enhanced by its landscaped gardens and stunning fountains.

(10) Algerian Sand Beach

The white sand of the 1.3-km- (1-mile-) long beach was imported from Algeria. A popular beach for swimming and cricket before Emirates Palace was built, it was felt the sand wasn't soft enough for royal feet.

(6) Domes

There are 114 domes here. The most stunning is the Grand Atrium dome, decorated with silver and gold glass mosaic tiles and a gold finial at its apex.

(7) Petrified Palm Trees

There are 8,000 trees within the hotel. Some of the palm trees have been petrified to preserve them forever. Ask at the reception to see them on a guided tour, available at AED 150 per person.

(8) Gold-Plated Lobby

The opulence of the lobby's gold interior **(left)** is dazzling. Until Emirates Palace was built, Abu Dhabi was a modest city. It was here that the city's wealth was ostentatiously put on display for the first time.

ON A SCALE LIKE NO OTHER

The Emirates Palace is spread over 1 million sq m (10 million sq ft), with over 300 rooms, around 2,000 staff from 50 different countries, 114 domes, 1,002 chandeliers, two helipads as well as a ballroom capable of accommodating more than 2,500 people. It is claimed even hotel staff sometimes get lost in the endless corridors.

TOP 10 ★ Desert Escapes

The Emirates' desert is sublime in parts and a trip here is incomplete without experiencing its myriad textures and colours. Not far out of the cities, camels graze on desert grass. If you don't have a 4WD and off-road driving skills, the best way to experience the desert is at the desert resorts Al Maha or Bab Al Shams. Or take a desert safari, which allows you to tick off a range of experiences you otherwise would not get a chance to do. If you have time, stay overnight, sleep under the stars and enjoy the silence.

LIWA OASIS

The most spectacular desert scenery can be enjoyed at Liwa Oasis, just a few hours drive from Abu Dhabi. The sand dunes here are the largest in the UAE. Beautifully coloured in pretty shades of peach and apricot, the sand dunes look at their best shortly after sunrise or just before sunset.

3 Ballooning

Drifting over the desert in a hot-air balloon **(right)** is an incredible experience. Balloon Adventures Dubai fly over the Dubai Desert Conservation Reserve.

1 Desert Safaris

Tour agencies such as Arabian Adventures organize desert safaris. Activities may include a thrilling drive in a 4WD, sand skiing, henna painting and sheesha, Arabic buffets and belly dancing.

4 Dubai Desert Conservation Reserve

Experience the unspoiled desert at this reserve, with dunes and rare wildlife, including oryx and mountain gazelle. Visit on a day tour or stay at the Al Maha resort.

5 Al Maha Resort

Book a romantic tent-like luxury suite *(see p117)*, and get your own plunge pool with the golden desert as your "backyard".

2 Bab Al Shams Desert Resort

The palm-shaded gardens and trickling ponds **(above)** make this resort *(see p117)* enchanting. A wonderful infinity pool overlooks the desert.

6 Belly Dancing

Belly dancing is known as Oriental Dancing in the Middle East, and it has a long history. Try to pick up some moves from the dancer at a desert safari – she may even pull you up for a dance.

8 Spectacular Stargazing

Book a desert astronomy session through tour companies like Platinum Heritage to learn about the wonders of the Arabian sky **(above)**. They offer guided nocturnal hikes and talks.

NEED TO KNOW

Arabian Adventures: open 9am–6pm; from AED 279; www.arabian-adventures.com

Balloon Adventures Dubai: 04 412 6333; open Sep–May; www.balloon-adventures.com

Dubai Desert Conservation Reserve: www.ddcr.og

Platinum Heritage: www.platinum-heritage.com

The Camel Farm: E77 northbound, between D63-Al Qudra Rd & E66-Al Ain Rd; 050 485 7676; www.thecamelfarm.ae

■ Desert temperatures are slightly cooler in spring, autumn and winter.

7 Bedouin Feast

Tuck into a delicious Arabic buffet, such as the Bedouin feast at Bab Al Shams' Al Hadheerah Desert Restaurant. You can experience local specialities including slow-roasted lamb ouzi.

9 Anantara Qasr al Sarab Resort

A secluded oasis nestled in the outskirts of Abu Dhabi, this retreat **(left)** has traditional hammams and outdoor pools, and exquisite Arabic food *(see p117)*. Unwind with arresting views of the desert, and dine under the stars.

10 Desert Camels

Trek through the sand dunes with a local guide, the way Bedouins once did with the stately, majestic camel **(above)**, a steadfast inhabitant of the desert. Visit the Camel Farm to learn more about how camels are cared for in the desert.

The Top 10
of Everything

The atrium at Burj Al Arab Jumeirah, Dubai

TOP 10 Moments in History

① **5110 BCE: Abu Dhabi settlement**

Artifacts tracing back to 5110 BCE have provided the first indications of human existence and habitation in Abu Dhabi. Examples of these include date stones found on Dalma Island, intricate flint tools from Merawah Island and the gravel plains of Al Ain.

② **700 CE: Islam arrives**

Conquests by the Umayyads, who established the second of the four major Islamic caliphates, led to the expansion of the Islamic faith throughout the Arabian Peninsula.

③ **1507: European traders reach the Gulf**

A Portuguese invasion to conquer Hormuz Island (known as Ormuz at the time) took place in 1507. The capture, led by Alfonso de Albuquerque, involved victories in Muscat, Kuryat and Khor Fakkan. It was also around this time that the famous Fortress of Ormuz was built. The invasion paved the way for Arabia to start trading with British, French and Dutch ships.

Portuguese-controlled Ormuz, a key trading centre

④ **1793: New Settlers arrive in Abu Dhabi**

The Al Bu Falah and Al Nahayan tribes settled in Abu Dhabi by 1793, attracted by its fertile soil and abundant wildlife.

These groups had roots in the Bedouin community of Bani Yas, a highly revered tribe from Southern Arabia.

⑤ **1833: Al Maktoum tribe arrives in Dubai**

Under the leadership of Maktoum bin Buti Al Maktoum, the Al Maktoum tribe settled at the mouth of Dubai Creek, establishing itself subsequently as one of the most prominent dynasties in the UAE. The family has ruled Dubai successfully ever since.

⑥ **1894: Tax-free trading**

Following a tempestuous fire that ravaged Deira in 1894, the city was rebuilt with the aid of prosperous businesses from abroad. Thereafter, Dubai's Sheikh Maktoum introduced complete tax exemptions and tax-free trading for foreign traders, giving birth to a period of economic successes. Persians were the first expats. They made their way to the Arab peninsula from the Persian Gulf, and later settled in Dubai. They were followed by traders from India, Europe and other neighbouring countries.

⑦ **1950s: The discovery and export of crude oil**

Oil was discovered in Abu Dhabi's Umm Shaif field in 1958, and in Dubai's offshore Fateh field in 1966. The fortunes of both the cities were immediately transformed with the subsequent oil drilling operations and export. The petroleum industry boomed, and with the massive increase in revenues, the region witnessed a significant upsurge in the number of schools, hospitals, buildings and roads built. There was also an extensive emphasis on construction and the development of city infrastructure. This brought about a tremendous change in the quality of life, and paved the way for a flourishing future ahead.

8 1971: UAE established

After the expiration of the British-Trucial Sheikhdoms treaty on 1 December 1971, the independent sheikhdoms signed the region's founding treaty, leading to a federal unification of the seven emirates. Sheikh Zayed bin Sultan Al Nahyan, ruler of Abu Dhabi, was sworn in as the new President of the UAE.

A replica of the Hope Probe

9 2020: Emirates Mars Mission

Led by the Mohammed Bin Rashid Space Centre, the United Arab Emirates Space Agency launched an uncrewed space exploration mission to Mars on 19 July 2020. Named the "Hope Probe", it went into orbit around Mars in February 2022 becoming the first probe to provide a complete picture of the Martian atmosphere and its layers.

10 2021: World Expo Dubai

Postponed due to the COVID-19 pandemic in 2020, the World Expo was eventually hosted by Dubai from 1 October 2021 to 31 March 2022, making it one of the world's first grand global gatherings since the pandemic struck. Expo City, a vast new infrastructural site was constructed for the event, which was attended by leaders from all over the world.

TOP 10 CULTURE AND TRADITION

1 Falconry
In the past, falcons were used by *Bedu* to capture small birds and hares. Today, Emirati men still train their falcons daily.

2 Traditional Dress
Women wear an *abaya* (a cloak-like dress) and a *shayla* (scarf). Men wear a *dishdasha* (robe) and a *gutra* (head scarf) with an *agal* (cord) to hold it in place.

3 The Camel
Camels were useful to the Bedouins for transporting heavy loads, for their milk and fur, which was used to make tents and textiles.

4 Fishing and the *Dhow*
Historically, fishing, pearl diving and building *dhows* (boats) were the main occupations along coastal settlements.

5 Bedouin Society
The Bedu tribes often spent the harsh summers inland at the cool oases and their winters fishing by the sea.

6 Poetry
Popular poetic forms include the romantic *baiti* style and the vernacular *nabati* poetry.

7 The Arabian Horse
The Arabian horse is one of the world's oldest and purest of breeds due to the Bedouins' careful breeding.

8 Pearling
Until the 1920s, this was Dubai's major source of income. By the 20th century the city had over 1,000 pearling boats.

9 The Date Palm
Dates, used for creating *tamr*, a preserve, were essential for desert survival. There are over 50 date varieties in the UAE.

10 Henna
Emirati women paint henna designs on their hands and feet for weddings and other events.

Henna designs being applied

TOP 10 Art Galleries

1 Jameel Arts Centre
MAP E2 ▪ Jaddaf Waterfront, Dubai ▪ 04 873 9800 ▪ Open 10am–8pm Mon, Wed, Thu, Sat & Sun (from noon Fri) ▪ www.jameelartscentre.org

Situated on Jaddaf Waterfront near the airport, this beautiful arts space hosts temporary exhibitions celebrating artists from across the UAE.

Abstact artwork at the Third Line

2 The Third Line
MAP C2 ▪ Warehouse 78 & 80, Street 8, Alserkel Ave, Al Quoz 1, Dubai ▪ 04 341 1367 ▪ Open 10am–7pm Sat–Thu; call ahead ▪ www.the thirdline.com

This gallery displays playful and edgy work by artists from around the Gulf. Exhibits change every couple of weeks.

3 Folklore Gallery
MAP Q2 ▪ Zayed 1st Street, Al Khalidiya, Abu Dhabi ▪ 02 666 0361 ▪ Open 9am–1pm & 4–9pm Sat–Thu ▪ www.folkloregallery.net

This is one of the best places to find works of art and craft from across the region, including handmade greeting cards, Turkish bookmarks, prints and even handblown glass.

4 Majlis Gallery
MAP K2 ▪ Al Musalla roundabout, Al Fahidi, Dubai ▪ 04 353 6233 ▪ Open summer: 10am–2pm Sat–Thu; winter: 10am–6pm Sat–Thu ▪ www.themajlis gallery.com

Dubai's oldest commercial art gallery (see p18) focuses on Arabian and Middle Eastern-themed work created by local and expat artists. Browse for good prints, ceramics and sculpture.

5 Efie Gallery
MAP C2 ▪ Unit 2, Al Khayat Art Avenue, 19th Street, Al Quoz 1 ▪ 04 252 4182 ▪ Open 11am–7pm Tue–Sun ▪ www.efiegallery.com

Using neighbouring Alserkal Avenue as a model, Dubai's Al Khayat Avenue is currently converting warehouses into art spaces. Efie Gallery was among the first to open with an exhibition by African artist El Anatsui, famous for his large-scale bottle-top installations, which have been displayed in New York's MOMA and the British Museum.

6 Green Art Gallery
MAP C2 ▪ Unit 28, Street 8, Alserkel Ave, Al Quoz 1, Dubai ▪ 04 346 9305 ▪ Open 10am–7pm Sat–Thu ▪ www.gagallery.com

Originally opened in Dubai in 1995 as an intimate salon d'art dedicated to Arab Modernism, this commercial

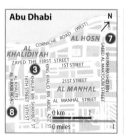

Kanoo exhibition of Pop Art at Tabari Artspace

gallery in Al Quoz displays the work of a multi-generational range of artists from the Middle East, North Africa, South Asia and beyond, with a focus on the heritage, cultures and environment of the Middle East. There is a programme of changing exhibitions throughout the year. These feature a diverse selection of media.

7 Abu Dhabi Art Hub

MAP U4 ■ Level 1, The Mall World Trade Center, Khalifa bin Zayed The First Street, Abu Dhabi ■ 02 551 5005 ■ Open 10am–10pm Sat–Fri ■ www.adah.ae

Focusing on both emerging and established visual artists, this gallery encourages interaction and cross-cultural artistic exchanges between national and international artists. Its sole purpose is to provide a cultural and educational service for emerging creative minds and established artists in the UAE.

8 Etihad Modern Art Gallery

MAP Q3 ■ Villa 15, Al Huwelat Street, Al Bateen, Abu Dhabi ■ 02 621 0145 ■ Open 10am–10pm Sat–Thu ■ www. etihadmodernart.com

A contemporary art gallery, which encourages the creation of art with local references. It exhibits the work of well-established and upcoming Emirati and international artists. The gallery also organizes art workshops, poetry nights and music events.

9 Tabari Artspace

MAP D6 ■ Gate Village, Building 3, Level 2, DIFC, Dubai ■ 04 323 0820 ■ Open 9am–6pm Sun–Thu ■ www. tabariartspace.com

With a mission to nurture local talent, this gallery hosts great exhibitions by Middle Eastern and Emirati artists, and attempts to bring into focus an understanding of borders, space, place and identity. Highlights include Mohammed Kanoo's playful Pop Art.

10 XVA

MAP K2 ■ Al Fahidi, Dubai ■ 04 353 5383 ■ Open 10am–6pm daily ■ www.xvagallery.com

This leading gallery *(see p19)* is set in a stylish boutique hotel in a restored traditional house. Its idyllic courtyard café also serves as an exhibition space.

The traditional exterior of XVA

🔟 Resorts in Dubai

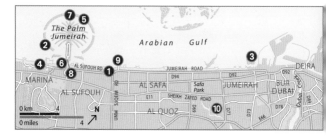

1 Jumeirah Al Qasr

Opulent to the last detail, this extravagant hotel looks almost like a Hollywood film set, with sweeping staircases, supersized chandeliers and lavish Arabian styling *(see p113)*. It is also where you will find the romantic Pierchic restaurant *(see p81)*, which offers memorable views of the nearby Burj Al Arab Jumeirah.

Jumeirah Zabeel Saray interior

2 Jumeirah Zabeel Saray

Dubai's fondness for extravagant interior design reaches fever pitch at this extraordinary Palm resort *(see p113)*, with a series of show-stopping restaurants and bars ranging from the stunning Indian-style restaurant Amala *(see p87)* to the Lebanese Al Nafoorah *(see p75)*.

3 Nikki Beach Resort & Spa

Straddling the waterfront of Pearl Jumeirah, this stylish resort is an urban oasis with spectacular views of the Arabian Gulf *(see p113)*. It is home to the popular Nikki Beach Club, known for its sheesha terrace and lounge, and a lovely bistro, Café Nikki, which offers delicious Friday brunches.

4 Ritz-Carlton Dubai

Traditional European design and understated elegance reign supreme at the superior Ritz-Carlton *(see p114)*. Savour the hotel's style over a sumptuous afternoon tea at the Lobby Lounge, sip cocktails in the opulent Library Bar, or enjoy a spot of pampering at the hotel's luxury spa.

5 Atlantis, The Royal

Dubai's ultra-luxury hotel *(see p113)* was dramatically unveiled in 2023 with an exclusive performance from Beyoncé. Designed by an elite team of artists and architects, the hotel and resort seeks to redefine sophisticated accommodation, with huge suites stacked in lavish blocks overlooking the Arabian Sea.

The decadent Atlantis, The Royal

several leading family attractions, including the Lost Chambers (see p83) and Aquaventure (see p84). Non-guests can also use the beautiful hotel beach.

The opulent One&Only Royal Mirage

⑧ FIVE Palm Jumeirah

This dazzling luxury resort is located in the Palm Jumeirah (see p113). Visit the chic rooftop pool, club and lounge, and The Penthouse for incredible drinks and charming sunsets. Enjoy the traditional Italian dishes created by Michelin-starred chef Giuseppe Pezzella, at the resort's popular Italian restaurant.

⑨ Burj Al Arab Jumeirah

No trip to Dubai is complete without a visit to the most famous building in the city – and perhaps the world. Enjoy a memorable afternoon tea in the dazzlingly decorated atrium or take in stunning views over a cocktail in the sky-high Skyview Bar (see pp24–5).

⑥ One&Only Royal Mirage

With Moorish-style buildings, Dubai's most romantic hotel is spread out along the beach amidst a forest of palms (see p113). Savour the atmosphere and explore the outstanding restaurants, including Eauzone (see p87) and Tagine (see p87), and relax in the stunning Oriental Spa.

⑦ Atlantis, The Palm

This towering arch-shaped resort (see p113) at the end of the Palm is one of the city's most famous landmarks and is also home to

⑩ The Palace Downtown

This hotel offers a haven of traditional Arabian style amidst the modern developments of Downtown Dubai (see p112). Visitors can admire the stunning lakeside setting, and enjoy a meal at the romantic Thiptara restaurant (see p75) or take afternoon tea in the decadent Al Bayt Lounge.

The ultra-luxurious Atlantis, The Palm resort, set amidst the Arabian Gulf

🔟 Outdoor Activities

Skydiving over the Palm Jumeirah

③ Wind Surfing

Great winds make Dubai an ideal wind-surfing destination. Most good beach resorts hire out equipment and also offer wind-surfing lessons. The Westin Mina Seyahi hotel (see p113) is particularly renowned for its facilities.

④ Fishing

Join an organized fishing trip where equipment is provided. Cook your fish on board or charter your own boat. Le Meridien Mina Seyahi Resort in Dubai (see p113) and the Beach Rotana in Abu Dhabi (see p116) offer great fishing trips.

① Skydiving

Skydive Dubai: MAP B1; Al Seyahi St, Dubai; 04 377 8888; www.skydivedubai.ae

For the ultimate Dubai high, strap yourself into a parachute and dive into the city. Skydive Dubai arrange tandem jumps over the Palm Jumeirah, and run a training school in the desert.

⑤ Dubai Autodrome

Dubai Autodrome Kartdrome: Emirates Rd, Dubai; MAP B3; 04 806 2220; www.dubaiautodrome.ae

Adrenaline-junkies can burn rubber driving pro-karts at the Dubai Autodrome. The Formula 1 standard racing circuit has 17 hair-raising turns. Book ahead for lessons at the excellent driving school.

② Scuba Diving

Emirates Diving Association: MAP D4; Jumeirah 1, Al Hudaiba Awards Buildings, Block B, 2nd Floor, Office 214; 04 393 9390; www.emiratesdiving.com

Racing car, the Autodrome

A popular local activity, the Emirates Diving Association offers information on diving in Dubai, Abu Dhabi and some of the East Coast towns.

⑥ Hot-air Ballooning

Getting a bird's-eye-view of the desert from a hot-air balloon (see p32) is simply sublime. Only by floating way above the dunes can you fully appreciate the waves of sand and patterns of light and sha-dow crafted by the ridges that are impossible to see from the ground.

A hot-air balloon floating over the desert landscape

(7) Wakeboarding

Al Forsan International Sports Resort: Khalifa City, St No. 12, Abu Dhabi; 02 656 5656; www.alforsan.com

Try your hand at some wakeboarding tricks on the Arabian Gulf sea. If you're a first-timer, the best place to learn is at a resort. Le Meridien Mina Seyahi Resort in Dubai (see p113) and the Al Forsan International Sports Resort in Abu Dhabi offer great lessons.

(8) Golfing

Dubai Golf: www.dubaigolf.com

Both Dubai and Abu Dhabi are awash with world-beating courses. Several international competitions take place every year, including the Omega Dubai Desert Classic at the city's largest course, the Emirates Golf Club.

Golfing at Omega Dubai Desert Classic

(9) Kite Surfing

Kite Beach: MAP C2; Jumeirah Beach, Dubai ▪ Duotone: Al Boom Marine, Jumeirah Rd, Dubai; 04 394 1258; www.duotonesports.com/kiteboarding

Join kite surfers on Kite Beach. Hire or buy equipment from Duotone, who will help you connect with instructors.

(10) Horseriding

Emirates Equestrian Centre: MAP D3; 050 558 7656 ▪ Abu Dhabi Equestrian Club: Al Ain, 050 558 7656

With its world-class equestrian centre, Dubai is the Middle East's undisputed horseriding capital. There is also a top equestrian centre in Abu Dhabi, which offers riding lessons.

TOP 10 SPECTATOR SPORTS

Runner in the Dubai Marathon

1 Dubai Marathon
Runners from all around the world compete on the city streets (see p53).

2 Omega Dubai Desert Classic
Watch the world's best golfers compete in this four-day tournament (see p53).

3 Dubai Duty Free Tennis Championships
See the big guns of world tennis serve action at Dubai Tennis Stadium (see p53).

4 Dubai Rugby Sevens
Nov ▪ www.dubairugby7s.com
The first leg of the Sevens World Tour is loved by rugby fans all over the world.

5 F1 Grand Prix
MAP W4 ▪ Yas Marina Circuit ▪ Nov ▪ www.yasmarinacircuit.com
Since 2009, Abu Dhabi has hosted a race at the Yas Marina circuit.

6 UAE Pro League
Winter weekday nights ▪ www.uaeproleague.ae/en
The choreographed dances and songs by the fans are just as riveting as the play on the field at this popular event.

7 Maktoum Rowing Cup
MAP B1 ▪ Dubai International Marine Club ▪ Dec ▪ www.dimc.ae
Sailing crews battle through Dubai's waters in traditional wooden rowing boats to win a prestigious trophy.

8 Powerboat Racing
Dec ▪ www.f1h2o.com
Watch the lightweight catamarans in action at this exciting race.

9 Dubai World Cup
Dress up for the world's richest horse race with a $6 million prize (see p53).

10 Abu Dhabi Desert Challenge
Bikes, 4WDs and even trucks take part in this international cross-country rally through the desert (see p53).

🔟 Children's Attractions

An exhilarating water slide at the Aquaventure water park

1 Magic Planet

MAP E2 ▪ Deira City Centre, Dubai ▪ 04 295 4333 ▪ Open 10am–11pm daily (until midnight Thu & Fri) ▪ Adm for rides ▪ www.deiracitycentre.com

An indoor entertainment venue for all the family, with a merry-go-round, bumper cars, pitch and putt golf, video games for children, and a soft-play area for toddlers.

2 Ski Dubai Snow Park

All ski levels and ages can try their hand at skiing or snowboarding on the slopes of the largest indoor snow park (see p77) in the world. There are also a variety of rides here, such as Bobsled, Tubing Run, Snow Bumpers, Zorb Ball 'Giant Ball' and Snow Plough Playground.

Watching the skiers at Ski Dubai

3 Aquaventure

Spread across 17 ha (43 acres) next to the Atlantis resort, this vast water park (see p84) has plenty to thrill visitors.

4 Dubai Parks and Resorts, Jebel Ali, Dubai

MAP B2 ▪ Sheikh Zayed Rd, Dubai Parks & Resorts, Dubai ▪ 04 820 0000 ▪ Open 11am–8pm daily (until 10pm Thu–Sat) ▪ Adm ▪ www.dubaiparksandresorts.com

Enjoy rides and shows based on the *Smurfs*, *Kung Fu Panda* and many other movies, at the Middle East's largest Hollywood-inspired theme park.

5 IMG Worlds of Adventure

MAP C3 ▪ Sheikh Mohammed Bin Zayed Rd, Dubai ▪ 04 403 8888 ▪ Open 11am–9pm daily (to 10pm Thu–Sat) ▪ Adm ▪ www.imgworlds.com

This large indoor amusement park is split into four themed zones, including two based on Marvel Comics and Cartoon Network.

6 Wild Wadi Water Park

MAP C3 ▪ Jumeira Rd, Dubai ▪ 04 348 4444 ▪ Opening hours vary, call ahead

Try some of the 30 adrenaline-fuelled watery rides or just float about on a rubber ring along the waterways of this enormous outdoor water park.

⑦ Yas Waterworld

MAP W4 ▪ Yas Island, Abu Dhabi
▪ 600 511115 ▪ Adm ▪ www.yaswater
world.com

With fun-filled activities for all ages,
this Emirati-themed water park has
45 rides, slides and other attractions.

⑧ Kidzania

MAP C6 ▪ Level 2, Dubai Mall,
Dubai ▪ 800 38224 6255 ▪ Open
10am–10pm daily (until 11pm Thu–
Sat) ▪ Adm; under 2s free ▪ www.
kidzania.ae

Young children take over the world at
Kidzania, a miniature city in which kids
can dress up in costumes and role-
play from a selection of different jobs,
including policeman and fireman.

The fun-filled Kidzania

⑨ Aventura® Parks

Mushrif Park, Dubai ▪ 052 178
7616 ▪ Open 10am–9pm Sun–Wed,
9am–10pm Thu–Sat ▪ Adm ▪ www.
aventuraparks.com

This adventure park, set in a natural
Ghaf tree forest, is scattered with
attractions for all levels and ages.
Apart from the famous 25 m (82 ft)
Tarzan jump, it also features bridges,
zip-lines and treetop activities.

⑩ Warner Bros. World™ Abu Dhabi

MAP W4 ▪ Yas Island, Abu Dhabi
▪ 600 511115 ▪ Open 10am–8pm daily
▪ Adm ▪ www.wbworldabudhabi.com

Immerse yourself in the world of
Warner Bros. characters and iconic
superheroes at this themed park.

TOP 10 PARKS, GARDENS AND BEACHES

Jumeirah Beach Park

1 Jumeirah Beach Park
This park has landscaped play areas
and a beach *(see p78)* with sunbeds.

2 Za'abeel Park
MAP F5–F6 ▪ Sheikh Zayed Rd, Dubai
A technology-themed park with a
football field, boating lake and cafés.

3 Al Seef Rd Park
MAP K2 ▪ Dubai
A great place to enjoy the creek action.

4 Creek Park
A huge botanical park *(see p16)* with
BBQ areas, a mini golf course and a
cable car.

5 Al Mamzar Beach Park
MAP F1 ▪ Al Hamriya, Dubai ▪ 04 296
6201 ▪ Open 8am–10pm; Mon is for
women and children (boys under 4)
only ▪ Adm
A child-friendly beach park with huge
picnic areas, four swimming beaches,
a mini train and bikes for hire.

6 Umm Suqeim Beach
MAP C2 ▪ Off Jumeirah Beach Rd,
Dubai
This public beach has shallow waters
and views of the Burj Al Arab Jumeirah.

7 Safa Park
A huge park *(see p77)* with lots to do.
Try the trampoline cage for fun.

8 Mushrif Park
MAP F3 ▪ Al Khawaneej Rd, Dubai
▪ Open 8am–10:30pm Sat–Wed,
8am–11:30pm Thu–Fri ▪ Adm
A desert park with pools, farm animals,
a theatre and a botanic garden.

9 La Mer Beach
MAP D2 ▪ 2 A St, Dubai
A sprawling, laidback beach with
an adventurous water park.

10 Kite Beach
MAP C2 ▪ Umm Suqeim, behind
Wollongong University, Dubai
A popular spot for watersports.

🔟 Best Bars in Dubai

Vivid blue and green decor at the popular Skyview Bar

① Skyview Bar

Located at the top of the Burj Al Arab Jumeirah, this is one of Dubai's ultimate places for a drink (see p24). Sweeping views up and down the coast are accompanied by a superior list of cocktails, wines and other drinks. Advance booking is required.

② The Rooftop

It is easy to fall in love with the magical look and feel of this atmospheric Moroccan-style rooftop bar (see p86), with its Arabesque lanterns and lounge music.

Moroccan styling at the Rooftop

③ Vault

At the top of the JW Marriott Marquis, Vault (see p74) is another head-in-the-clouds bar with amazing views across Dubai. Chic decor and cocktails attract a monied crowd.

④ Bar 44

Prop yourself up at the swanky circular bar or sink into a plush chair at this swish cocktail bar (see p86) on level 44 (hence the name) of the Grosvenor House hotel. It attracts a regular sophisticated local set as well as visiting businesspeople out to impress colleagues with spectacular views over the bustling Dubai Marina.

⑤ Mr. Miyagi's

An eclectic bar and restaurant offering great music, stylish cocktails, and the best Asian street flavours in the city, Mr. Miyagi's (see p86) is hailed as one of the best bars in Dubai. It has quirky interiors and a whimsical menu of drinks ranging from Komodo Dragons to Ting Tongs. Be sure to try their delicious selection of bao buns, dim sums, and sushi rolls.

⑥ Asia Asia

Ranking high on various lists of the world's very best bars, this glamorous establishment (see p74) features a glittering canopy of stars and expertly crafted cocktails. The bar's Cosmic Menu features inventive cocktails inspired by constellations.

7 Nola

With a menu inspired by cuisine from New Orleans, Nola *(see p86)* bustles with life every evening. A diverse array of delicious cocktails and Southern American dishes is served here, and the fun vibe is perfectly complemented by the vintage interiors, friendly service, and the weekly live music performances.

8 At.Mosphere

On the 122nd floor of the Burj Khalifa, this *(see p75)* is the world's highest bar, offering jaw-dropping views in swanky surroundings. Most people come to eat in the attached restaurant here, but you can also book youself in for a drink. Advance reservations are required.

9 Bahri Bar

You'll be impressed with the enchanting old-Arabian details and sumptuous interiors of the colonial-styled bar *(see p81)* at the Mina A'Salam hotel. Nurse a drink on the veranda and take in the mesmerizing view of the Burj Al Arab Jumeirah.

Views from the veranda, Bahri Bar

10 Weslodge

Rock-and-roll meets refined elegance at this chic bar and restaurant.With a selection of classic drinks reinterpreted with an inventive twist, and the best North American cuisine in the city, Weslodge *(see p74)* offers a great escape for party-goers and bar hoppers in Dubai.

TOP 10 SHEESHA SPOTS

Shimmers, located on the beach

1 Shimmers
MAP C2 ▪ Madinat Jumeirah, Dubai ▪ 04 432 3232 ▪ Open noon–11:30pm daily
Sheesha at a deluxe beach shack.

2 Kan Zaman
Smoke under the stars at this Arabic café *(see p69)* by the creek.

3 The Courtyard
MAP B1 ▪ One&Only Royal Mirage Hotel, Jumeirah, Dubai ▪ 04 399 9999 ▪ Open 7pm–1am daily
A great selection of aromatic tobacco blends in a cushion-strewn courtyard.

4 Shakespeare & Co
MAP D4 ▪ The Village Mall, Dubai ▪ 04 344 6228 ▪ Open 7am–1am daily
A French Baroque-style patisserie by day, and a sheesha bar at night.

5 Souk Madinat Jumeirah
The central plaza is a breezy, magical spot *(see p80)* to smoke sheesha.

6 QDs
Expats love this great smoking spot *(see p62)* overlooking the creek.

7 Barouk
MAP E5 ▪ Crowne Plaza, Yas Island, Abu Dhabi ▪ 02 656 3064 ▪ Open 6pm–1am daily
A Lebanese café with a sheesha terrace.

8 Khan Murjan
MAP E2 ▪ Wafi City, Dubai ▪ 04 327 9795 ▪ Open 9am–12:30am daily
The grandeur of a 14th- century souk, in the heart of Modern Dubai.

9 Buhayra Lounge
MAP D2 ▪ Palace Downtown, Sheikh Mohammed bin Rashid Blvd, Dubai ▪ 04 288 8396 ▪ Open 8–1am daily
Enjoy a mix of drinks and music at this pool-side lounge.

10 Balcon Terrace
MAP T1 ▪ Southern Sun Abu Dhabi, Mina Rd, Abu Dhabi ▪ Open 3pm–1am daily
A rooftop pool bar serving sheesha.

🔟 Restaurants

1 Zuma

With branches in both Abu Dhabi and Dubai, this fine-dining restaurant *(see p95)* offers modern Japanese cuisine made with a twist. Try out their *robata* grill and also the sushi counter which celebrates the traditional Japanese *Izakaya* style of informal eating and drinking. It also serves great cocktails and signature nigiri and maki rolls.

The lively and atmospheric Zuma

2 Pitfire Pizza

Arguably Dubai's favourite pizza joint, Pitfire *(see p87)* serves a large range of pizzas which combine Neapolitan traditions with New York creativity. The restaurant also serves pastas and salads.

3 Bord Eau

French fine dining is the theme at this upmarket restaurant *(see p101)* housed in Abu Dhabi's Shangri-La Hotel. Opt for the exciting blind-tasting menu, and choose between a seat in the beautiful old-world dining room or on the terrace outside.

4 Nusr-Et Steakhouse

Founded by Nusret Gökçe, known popularly across the internet as Salt Bae, this steakhouse *(see p81)* has excellent ambience and service, and an exceptional menu that is both simple as well as tasteful. A haven for meat lovers, it features wholesome burgers, lamb fillets and fillet mignon steaks, and delicious beef tenderloins, among other delightful treats.

5 COYA Dubai

This award-winning gem of a venue *(see p81)* celebrates Incan heritage with a contemporary selection of Peruvian dishes. Inspired by the vibrant Latin American culture, COYA Dubai serves fusion cuisine from Peru with a modern twist and meticulously accented with Japanese, Chinese and Spanish elements.

6 Eauzone

Located in the One&Only Royal Mirage *(see p113)*, this is one of Dubai's most romantic restaurants *(see p87)*. Visit after dark and dine at tables in miniature Arabian tents set between floodlit pools. The food features top-quality Pan-Asian cuisine including some traditional classics and delicious contemporary fusion creations.

Eauzone, set beside a floodlit pool

A table setting at Indego by Vineet

⑦ Indego by Vineet
Vineet Bhatia, India's first Michelin-starred chef, showcases his unique talents at this stylish restaurant (see p87). It offers a mix of traditional Indian favourites along-side more unusual contemporary creations, blending European and subcontinental influences.

⑧ Hoi An
The aesthetic of colonial-era French Indochina lives on at these beautiful wood-panelled restaurants, located in the Shangri-La Hotel in both Dubai (see p75) and Abu Dhabi (see p101). The menu offers delicious Vietnamese–French cuisine.

⑨ Rhodes Twenty10
The legacy of the late British celebrity chef Gary Rhodes endures at this elegant restaurant serving Rhodes' signature reworkings of traditional British classics alongside a selection of more Middle Eastern-influenced creations.

⑩ Hoseki
A Michelin-starred Japanese restaurant (see p81) serving the stunning creations of chef Masahiro Sugiyama. Diners are seated at the counter, as the chef devises dishes tailored to the preferences of each individual guest.

TOP 10 MIDDLE EASTERN RESTAURANTS

1 Tagine
An exquisitely decorated restaurant (see p87) serving fine Moroccan cuisine.

2 Lebanese Flower
Abu Dhabi residents flock to this excellent Lebanese restaurant (see p95).

3 Zahr el Laymoun
MAP B6 ▪ Souk Al Bahar, Dubai ▪ 04 242 3366 ▪ Open 10am–midnight ▪ www.zahrellaymoun.com ▪ DD
Enjoy good Lebanese cuisine at this place overlooking the Dubai Fountain.

4 Shabestan
MAP L2 ▪ Radisson Blu Hotel, Dubai Creek ▪ 04 222 7171 ▪ Open 12:30–3:30pm & 7:30–11:30pm ▪ DDD
Expect quality Iranian cuisine and creek views at this hotel restaurant.

5 Awtar
MAP E2 ▪ Grand Hyatt Dubai, Dubai ▪ 04 317 2221 ▪ Open 7:30pm–3am Sun–Fri ▪ DDD
This place offers good Lebanese food with regular bellydancing performances.

6 Al Nafoorah
Top-quality Lebanese cuisine is served in a sedate setting (see p75).

7 Almaz by Momo
A Moroccan café (see p81) owned by restaurateur Mourad "Momo" Mazouz.

8 Bastakiah Nights
A lovely courtyard restaurant (see p19) in a beautiful old Al Fahidi mansion.

9 Al Fanar
MAP E3 ▪ Ground Floor, Dubai Festival City ▪ 02 656 0600 ▪ Open 9am–10pm daily ▪ www.alfanarrestaurant.com/uae ▪ DD
This family restaurant celebrates innovative Emirati cuisine.

10 Arabian Tea House Café
Affordable Arabian fare is served in a pretty courtyard garden (see p69).

Arabian Tea House Café

⭐🔟 Shopping Malls and Souks

Textiles for sale, Souk Al Bahar

① Souk Al Bahar
Just over the waterway from the Dubai Mall is this more Arabic-themed affair *(see p72)* featuring an array of boutique and antique shops. There is also an excellent selection of restaurants and bars.

② Mall of the Emirates
Over 520 stores, including a swish Harvey Nichols, make this the city's most sumptuous mall *(see p79)* If you're in a rush, use the mall's website to create an itinerary identifying the most direct route to the shops you wish to visit.

③ Mirdif City Centre
MAP E3 ■ Sheikh Mohammed Bin Zayed Rd ■ 800 6422 ■ Open 10am–midnight daily ■ www.city centremirdif.com
This mall has designer boutiques, several eateries, and entertainment options for both adults and children, including a sleek IMAX movie theatre and the very popular Magic Planet.

④ Dubai Festival City
MAP E3 ■ Al Rebat St, Dubai ■ 800 332 ■ Open 10am–10pm Sun–Wed, 10am–midnight Thu–Sat
Located by the waterfront, the Dubai Festival City offers a French Riviera-style marina, excellent shopping and alfresco dining. Its 400 shops include a huge Marks & Spencer and an IKEA.

⑤ Marina Mall (Abu Dhabi)
With over 300 shops, expect big name brands, exclusive stores such as Rolex and Tiffany & Co, and traditional Arabian perfume, sweets and clothes shops. Excellent cafés here *(see p91)* include Hediard from Paris.

⑥ Wafi City
A quirky mall *(see p68)* adorned with pharaonic statues, miniature pyramids and hieroglyphics. Shops include independent fashion boutiques and the Wafi Gourmet deli.

Mall of the Emirates, crowned by an impressive glass dome

7 Abu Dhabi Mall

Generally considered to be Abu Dhabi's smartest mall, this place *(see p94)* has a wide array of shops. You can find stores for everything from designer fashion to electronics and home furnishings.

8 Ibn Battuta Mall

MAP A2 ■ Sheikh Zayed Rd ■ 800 625 4335 ■ Open 10am–10pm daily ■ www.ibnbattutamall.com/en

Named after the famous explorer, this themed shopping centre in Dubai has over 275 retailers spread across six courts. The decor for each area is inspired by the countries that Ibn Battuta, travelled to: Tunisia, Egypt, Persia, India, Andalucia and China. There is also a 21-screen cinema.

Ibn Battuta's exotic interior

9 The Galleria

Set across three floors, the Galleria *(see p94)*, one of Abu Dhabi's newest consumer additions, houses numerous boutique stores owned by world-class luxury brands.

10 The Dubai Mall

Next to the world's biggest tower sits the world's largest shopping mall *(see p73)*. This monument to consumerism houses over 1,000 stores, not to mention an ice rink, an aquarium, and a vast cinema and entertainment complex. The mall also has more than 150 food outlets, offering everything from fine dining to casual restaurants. For Emiratis, the Dubai Mall is as much about socializing as it is about shopping.

TOP 10 THINGS TO BUY

A selection of traditional *khanjars*

1 Arabian handicrafts
Collectible local handicrafts include traditional Arabian-style coffeepots, traditional *khanjars* (daggers) and miniature carved wooden boxes.

2 Carpets
Numerous shops across the UAE sell opulent Persian carpets at prices significantly lower than you would pay back home. Make sure you bargain hard.

3 Perfume
Concoct your own scent from Arabian oils *(attar)* in a local perfume shop.

4 Gold and gems
Gold prices in Dubai are amongst the cheapest found anywhere in the world, while precious stones (diamonds in particular) are also very keenly priced.

5 Fun souvenirs
Mosque-shaped alarm clocks, cuddly camels and Burj Khalifa paperweights all make enjoyable mementos.

6 Camel Milk Chocolate
High in natural fats, local camel milk makes extra rich and creamy chocolate.

7 Bedouin jewellery
Chunky antique silver bangles, necklaces and rings make unusual but affordable souvenirs.

8 Music
Stock up on a selection of recordings of Middle Eastern music, from more traditional Emirati singers to Egyptian and Lebanese pop megastars.

9 Aladdin slippers
Dress like Aladdin in a pair of curly-toed Arabian slippers.

10 Electronics
Keen competition keeps prices low for mobiles, laptops and tablets.

🔟 Dubai and Abu Dhabi for Fre

The striking white façade of Sheikh Zayed Mosque, a principal religious site

1 Sculpture Gardens

Dubai Creek is the atmospheric backdrop of Jameel Arts Centre's sculpture gardens (see p38). Inside you'll find a roster of contemporary exhibitions that are free to attend, as well as a library dedicated to artists.

2 Free Museums

Museum admission rarely costs more than a few dirhams, but some places – including Dubai's Coffee Museum (see p18), the Traditional Architecture Museum (see p67), Heritage House (see p59), Al-Ahmadiya School (see p59) and the Abu Dhabi Heritage Village (see p92) – are completely free.

Exhibits at the Coffee Museum

3 Sheikh Zayed Mosque

Abu Dhabi's single biggest tourist attraction (see pp28–9) is absolutely free to enter – and there are even gratis guided tours.

4 Walk the Boardwalk

Take a stroll along the boardwalk at Palm Jumeirah (see p82). Look out for the remarkable array of luxury resorts that are popping up along the waterfront, best appreciated at sunset, when the hotels become silhouettes on the horizon.

5 Art for Free

Dubai's many art galleries (see pp38–9) offer endless scope for seeing the work of leading Middle Eastern and other artists at zero cost – unless you want to take a piece home.

6 Amazing Malls

Some of Dubai's malls are virtual tourist attractions in their own right. Top picks include the extrava-gantly decorated Ibn Battuta Mall (see p83) and the upscale Mall of the Emirates (see p79), which has surreal views of the snow-clad slopes of Ski Dubai (see p77), complete with the occasional penguin.

7 Waterside Walks

The breezy walks along the Bur Dubai side (south) of the creek (see pp16–17) in Dubai and along the Abu Dhabi Corniche (see p90) are spectacular. You'll see some of the best sights in these intriguing cities and it won't cost you a penny.

8 Free Beaches

The huge sandy beach at the Dubai Marina (see p84) is a popular local destination, with plenty of facilities available, including water sports. In Abu Dhabi, there's a fine stretch of free soft white sand and clear blue sea fringing the city's beautiful Corniche (see p90).

9 Ras Al Khor Wildlife Sanctuary

Settle into a hide and watch colourful flocks of bright pink flamingos and other birds (see p72) framed against a surreal backdrop of skyscrapers. It is free to use the hides but groups of 10 or more require a permit.

Ras Al Khor Wildlife Sanctuary

10 Dubai Fountain

Dubai's record-breaking choreographed fountain, (see p71) set in the middle of Burj Khalifa Lake, can be enjoyed for free every evening and most afternoons from any part of the broad pedestrianized walkway running around the lake. This must-see experience offers close-up views of the dancing jets and watery swirls as they rise up, accompanied by dramatic music.

TOP 10 FESTIVALS AND EVENTS

Dubai Shopping Festival

1 Dubai Marathon
Jan ▪ www.dubaimarathon.org
An annual marathon race across the city.

2 Dubai Duty Free Tennis Championships
MAP E2 ▪ Dubai Duty Free Tennis Stadium ▪ Feb–Mar ▪ www.dubai dutyfreetennischampionships.com
Players battle it out at this tennis event.

3 Dubai World Cup
MAP D3 ▪ Meydan racetrack ▪ Feb–Mar ▪ www.dubaiworldcup.com
The world's richest horse-racing cup.

4 Art Dubai
MAP C2 ▪ Madinat Arena ▪ Mar ▪ www.artdubai.ae
Dubai's biggest contemporary art fair.

5 Dubai International Jazz Festival
MAP B2 ▪ Dubai Media City ▪ Mar ▪ www.dubaijazzfest.com
Crowds gather for performances by the world's biggest jazz names.

6 Omega Dubai Desert Classic
MAP B2 ▪ Mar ▪ www.dubaidesert classic.com
A renowned golf tournament.

7 Abu Dhabi Desert Challenge
Apr ▪ www.abudhabidesert challenge.com
A 4-day motor rally through the desert.

8 Dubai International Film Festival
MAP C2 ▪ Madinat Jumeirah ▪ Dec ▪ www.dubaifilmfest.com
Enjoy glam galas and film screenings.

9 Dubai Shopping Festival
Citywide ▪ Dec–Feb ▪ www.mydsf.ae
A retail and entertainment extravaganza.

10 Global Village
MAP C3 ▪ Dubailand, Emirates Rd ▪ Dec–Feb ▪ www.globalvillage.ae
A fun-filled multicultural bazaar.

🔟 Excursions and Tours

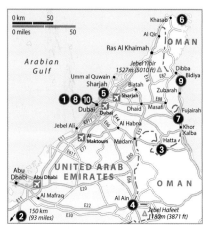

3 Hatta

105 km (65 miles) from Dubai ▪ Heritage Village: open 8am–7:30pm Sat–Thu, 3–9pm Fri

Visit the Heritage Village at this serene oasis town. A drive into the mountains from here leads to the clear Hatta Rock Pools, a fantastically beautiful spot for swimming.

4 Al Ain

160 km (99 miles) from Dubai ▪ Al Ain Palace Museum: 03 711 8388 ▪ Jahili Fort: next to Al Ain Rotana Hotel ▪ Al Ain Camel Souk: Al Ain-Buraimi border

Known as Garden City, this green emirate is home to the Al Ain Palace Museum. Also here are the Al Ain Livestock Souk and the Jahili Fort.

1 Wonder Bus Tour

04 359 5656 ▪ www.wonderbusdubai.net

This one-hour tour starts with a drive down to Shindagha in Bur Dubai, at which point the vehicle plunges into the creek for a cruise through the old city before returning to land.

2 Liwa

300 km (186 miles) from Abu Dhabi

Liwa's high golden dunes (see p32) are almost devoid of vege-tation. Yet, date-producing farms flourish close by, creat-ing an awesome spectacle.

Liwa's sandswept roads

Pot, Heritage Museum, Sharjah

5 Sharjah

10 km (6 miles) from Dubai ▪ Sharjah Art Museum: 06 568 8222 ▪ Heritage Museum: 06 568 0006 ▪ Archaeological Museum: 06 566 5466

The Heritage Museum, the Sharjah Art Museum and the Archaeological Museum are must-see sights. The souks here are also very good for shopping.

Rugged mountain scenery on the Musandam Peninsula

⑥ Musandam Peninsula

193 km (120 miles) from Dubai ■ Khasab Travel & Tours: www.khasabtours.com ■ Visa available at Oman entry point

With amazing mountain cliffs and a coastline of inlets and fjords, this northerly enclave is part of Oman. Enjoy *dhow* day-trips into the fjords.

⑦ Fujairah

130 km (81 miles) from Dubai

Fujairah has a coastline of coral reefs and hillsides with forts and watchtowers. The Fujairah Fort is the oldest in the UAE, dating to 1670.

⑧ The Yellow Boats

www.theyellowboats.com

For the best views of the modern city, head out on the water with the Yellow Boats. Tours run up and down the coast starting from Dubai Marina, offering superlative views of the Marina skyscrapers, Atlantis and the Palm, and the Burj Al Arab Jumeirah.

⑨ Bidiya

38 km (24 miles) north of Fujairah ■ Visit outside of prayer times, accompanied by a mosque guide

This tiny fishing village is home to the oldest mosque in the UAE, dating back to 1446. Made from mud brick, stone and gypsum, it is now restored, with its four small domes held up by a massive central pillar.

Bidiya's 15th-century mosque

⑩ Al Fahidi Walking Tour

Tours: Tue, Thu, Sat & Sun

Explore Dubai's historic and atmospheric Al Fahidi district with an expert guide from the Sheikh Mohammed Centre for Cultural Understanding *(see p18)*. The 90-minute morning tours also include a rare chance to see inside the neighbouring Diwan Mosque and are followed by a Q&A session.

Dubai and Abu Dhabi Area by Area

Towering skyscrapers lining
the spectacular Dubai Marina

𝗧𝗢𝗣 𝟭𝟬 Deira

Gold Souk goods

Deira is the bustling commercial area north of Dubai Creek. It is the source of Dubai's trading roots and it is around the creek that you really get a palpable sense of its origins. There is a telling contrast between the sight of the old wooden *dhows* moored at the wharfside and the glass façades of the sleek skyscrapers that surround them. Much of the *dhow* cargo is destined for the souks and shopping districts of buzzy Deira. As a result, the narrow streets here have some of Dubai's most atmospheric souks, including the Gold Souk, Spice Souk and Grand Souk Deira. A major preservation effort by Dubai Municipality means that this area offers some architectural gems like the Al-Ahmadiya School and the Heritage House.

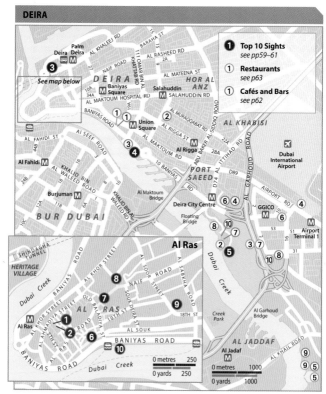

DEIRA

- ❶ **Top 10 Sights** see pp59–61
- ① **Restaurants** see p63
- ① **Cafés and Bars** see p62

Courtyard at Heritage House

1 Heritage House
MAP K1 ■ Al Khor St ■ 800
33222 ■ Open 8am–7:30pm Sat–Thu,
2:30–7:30pm Fri

This beautifully restored airy
courtyard house dates back to the
1890s. Unusually, this 10-room
building does not have a windtower,
but the upper floor is designed with
open doors and windows to draw in
the creek breezes. Now a museum
giving an insight into Emirati history
(with dioramas and touch screens),
you can explore the different rooms,
all with 19th-century furnishings.

2 Al Ahmadiya School
MAP K1 ■ Al Khor St ■ 800
33222 ■ Open 8am–7:30pm Sat–Thu,
2:30–7:30pm Fri

Dubai's first school, opened in 1912,
was founded by a philanthropist pearl
merchant. Mathematics, the Holy
Koran and Arabic calligraphy were
taught, and the pupils (all male) sat
on palm mats. Many such schools
were located in Emirati coastal
cities with the support of leading
merchants and sheikhs, who sub-
sidised the education. This school
closed in 1963. Now a museum, it
offers a great educational insight
into the past and is worth visiting
just for its sheer architectural grace.

3 Waterfront Market
The sights and smells of a
traditional food market provide an
enthralling insight into the shopping
and eating habits of the locals. On
the north side of Deira, this large
warehouse-like complex (see p27)
is the old city's major source of fresh
food. The colourful fruit and vege-
table selection has dozens of stalls
piled high with produce, as well as
a section specializing in dates from
the local area. The gory meat section
is for dedicated carnivores only,
while the fish and seafood section
has over 350 seasonal varieties of
seafood including ocean-fresh
prawns, hammour and sharks.

4 Emirates National Bank of Dubai
MAP L1 ■ Baniyas Rd

Another architectural achievement
is the building housing the Emirates
National Bank of Dubai – one of the
city's first iconic buildings. Built in
the mid-1990s by Carlos Ott, architect
of the Opéra de la Bastille in Paris,
it is inspired by the *dhow*. Its curved
curtain glass wall symbolizes the
billowing sail. Its base is clad in green
glass, representing water, and its
roof is cast in aluminium (denoting
the hull of the boat). It is most
striking at sunset, when
the mirror reflects
its gold and
silver lights.

**Emirates
National Bank
of Dubai's
stunning
façade**

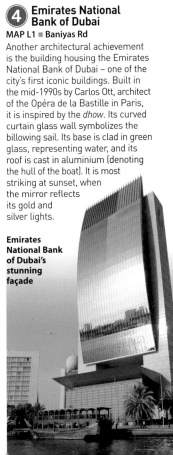

The beautifully manicured greens of the Dubai Creek Golf and Yacht Club

5 Dubai Creek Golf and Yacht Club

MAP E2 ■ Garhoud ■ 04 295 6000

This soaring white building, inspired by the sails of a *dhow* and sitting amidst rolling greens, is a city landmark, visible from both Maktoum and Garhoud bridges. Opened in January 1993, the world-class golf course here is the centrepiece of a sprawling leisure complex that also incorporates a 115-berth marina. The separate yacht club incorporates the Aquarium, an excellent seafood restaurant, as well as one of Dubai's most popular alfresco restaurants, the Boardwalk *(see p63)*, which sits on stilts and offers a spectacular view of the creek, especially at night when the illuminated *dhows* pass by.

6 Spice Souk

Moody and atmospheric, the Spice Souk *(see p27)* is a sensory trip into the past, where you can wander

Exotic spices at the Spice Souk

through a maze of narrow alleyways of shops piled high with aromatic spices. Take an *abra* (water taxi) to the souk, where you'll find sacks of cinnamon sticks, cumin, coriander seed and oud. Some great souvenir buys include frankincense, henna kits (for hand and body decoration), saffron and fragrant rose water.

DEIRA HISTORY

Liberal trade policies have backed the development of Deira, which had become the largest souk on the Arabian coast by the early 20th century. It was a haven for merchants who left Lingah, on the Persian coast, after high customs were introduced there in 1902. They continued to trade with Lingah, as do many of the *dhows* in the creek.

---

7 Perfume Souk

Immediately east of the Gold Souk, Sikkat al Khail Rd is home to an array of shops popularly known as the Perfume Souk *(see p27)* – although there isn't any actual souk building. Dozens of small shops line the street, selling a mix of international brands and local perfumes. The best are made using the aromatic oud (derived from aloe wood) and come in ornate cut-glass bottles. Most shops also allow you to create your own scents from their selection of perfume oils.

8 Gold Souk

You are unlikely to have ever seen so much gleaming gold as in Dubai's historic Gold Souk *(see p26)*. The souk is still dominated by Indian and Iranian craftsmen and traders, as it has been for close on a century. It has been restored with a traditional Arabic arcade and an arching wooden roof. You'll find jewellery in both Arabic and western styles.

9 Grand Souk Deira

This is where you get a real taste of the melting pot of cultures that is Dubai. The souk *(see p26)* is frequented by both Emiratis and expats, and sells such things as bright Indian clothing, perfumes, herbs and spices, colourful shawls and fabrics. It is a fascinating area to wander around.

Colourful textiles, Deira Covered Souk

10 Dhow Wharfage

MAP L1 ■ Baniyas Rd

A walk along the wharfside beside Baniyas Road allows you to get up close to the painted wooden *dhows*, the traditional Arabian sailing vessels moored here. These ships still trade around the Gulf. Their cargo these days is tyres, refrigerators, air conditioners, electronics – just about any modern item. Moored five or six abreast, these *dhows* have sailed to trade with Dubai from places such as Pakistan and Sudan since the 1830s.

A STROLL THROUGH THE SOUKS

> **AFTERNOON**

Aim to start this walk around 4:30pm, when the souk shops re-open after prayers and temperatures are cooler. Start with an *abra* crossing *(see pp16–17)* from the **Bur Dubai Abra Station**. You can disembark at Deira Old Souk Abra Station. Take the underpass beneath Baniyas Road to emerge at the **Spice Souk** entrance. Enjoy a browse among the fragrant alleyways here. Leave the Spice Souk at Al-Abra St, turn right along Al-Ras St, which leads into Sikkat Al-Khail St. Ahead you will see the latticed entrance to the **Gold Souk**, with its colonnaded interior. There are more than 300 jewellery shops to explore (most accept credit cards).

Wander into the narrow alleyways off the main thoroughfare and enjoy a traditional cup of tea at one of the small cafés.

Exit at the Gold Souk and continue along Sikkat Al-Khail St to the tiny **Perfume Souk**. The shop windows here are a treasure trove of bottles filled with heady Arabian scents, incense and oud.

EVENING

Continue along Sikkat Al-Khail St and enjoy an evening snack at **Ashwaq Cafeteria** *(04 226 1164)*, a down-to-earth café with outdoor tables, serving shwarmas. Next, return to the creek to admire the **Dhow Wharfage**. For a relaxed ending to the day, drop in at Dubai Creek and Yacht Club's **QDs** *(see p62)* and chill out with a cocktail.

See map on p58 ←

Cafés and Bars

1 YUM!

MAP L2 ▪ Radisson Blu Hotel ▪ 04 205 7033 ▪ Open noon–11pm daily ▪ D

"Live Fast: East Fast" is this noodle kitchen's motto. Inspired by different Far Eastern cuisines, it makes for a fun pit stop for lunch or a quick dinner.

2 Aroos Damascus

MAP L3 ▪ Al Muraqqabat Rd ▪ 04 221 3673 ▪ Open 7am–3am daily ▪ D

One of the city's best cheap Middle Eastern cafés, with a menu featuring mezze, grills and fish, all beautifully cooked. Try to get a table on the terrace.

3 Ashiana Restaurant

MAP K3 ▪ Sheraton Dubai Creek ▪ 04 207 1733 ▪ Open noon–3:30pm & 6:30–11pm daily ▪ DD

Aptly named (Ashiana means "home"), this Indian fine-dining restaurant serves Awadhi soul food.

4 PappaRoti

MAP E2 ▪ 04 2999266 ▪ Deira City Centre ▪ Open 9am–11pm Sun–Thu (until midnight Fri & Sat) ▪ D

Try crisp, golden-crusted buttered buns, and delicious beverages including teas, flavoured coffees, juices and more at this restaurant. PappaRoti is ideal for a quick nibble while you're catching a break from touring the city.

5 Eclipse Bar

MAP E3 ▪ InterContinental, Dubai Festival City ▪ 04 701 1111 ▪ Open 6pm–2am Sat–Wed, 6pm–3am Thu & Fri ▪ DD

This cocktail bar has the wow factor thanks to its views over Dubai Creek.

6 Paul

MAP E2 ▪ Deira City Centre ▪ 04 295 8404 ▪ Open 9am–11pm daily ▪ DD

This bustling French brasserie chain has taken the city by storm over the past few years. It has excellent sandwiches, salads and eggs Benedict.

7 Cielo Sky Lounge

MAP E2 ▪ Dubai Creek Golf & Yacht Club ▪ 04 416 1801 ▪ Opening hours vary; call ahead ▪ DD

A terrace bar with magnificent views of the Dubai skyline. Whether you're looking to grab a sundowner or a fun night of music and dance, Cielo is the ideal spot for partygoers.

8 Irish Village

MAP E2 ▪ Garhoud ▪ 04 282 4750 ▪ Open 11am–1am Sat–Wed, 11am–2am Thu & Fri ▪ DD

Throw back a pint and tuck into some fish and chips in Guinness batter at this Irish-style pub. The outdoor bench seating is an added delight.

9 Belgian Beer Café

MAP E3 ▪ Crown Plaza, Dubai Festival City ▪ 04 701 1127 ▪ Open 12:30pm–2am daily ▪ DD

A favourite among expats, the BBC, as it is affectionately known, offers a wide range of Belgian speciality ales and traditional dishes.

10 QD's

MAP K6 ▪ Dubai Creek and Yacht Club ▪ 04 295 6000 ▪ Open 5pm–2am daily ▪ DD

Lounge with a sundowner at this creekside wooden-decked terrace bar or enjoy a sheesha at the *majlis* area while the live band plays.

The open-air terrace bar at QD's

Restaurants

1 The China Club
MAP L2 ■ Radisson Blu Hotel
■ 04 222 7171 ■ Open 12:30–3pm &
7–11pm daily ■ DD
This elegant restaurant has striking
Chinese decor and an extensive menu
of dim sum and Chinese classics.

The stylish interior of the China Club

2 Twiggy By La Cantine
MAP E2 ■ Park Hyatt Hotel,
Dubai Creek Golf Club ■ 04 602 1105
■ Open 9am–2am daily ■ DDD
Set on an artificial lagoon over-
looking Dubai Creek, this restaurant
specializes in Mediterranean cuisine.

3 Thai Kitchen
MAP E2 ■ Park Hyatt Hotel,
Dubai Creek Golf Club ■ 04 602 1814
■ Open 7pm–midnight Sat-Thu, 12:30–
4pm & 7pm–midnight Fri ■ DD
Thai delicacies are served from live
cooking areas. The tasting portions
allow you to sample a range of dishes.

4 Seafood Market
MAP E2 ■ Le Meridien Dubai
Hotel & Conference Center, Airport Rd
■ 04 702 2455 ■ Open 12:30–5pm &
7–11:30pm daily ■ DD
This seafood restaurant is revered
for its fresh fish presented on ice.

5 Cheesecake Factory
MAP E2 ■ Dubai Festival City
Mall ■ 04 419 0874 ■ Open 10am–11pm
Sun–Wed (until midnight Thu–Sat) ■ DD
A truly hearty, indulgent restaurant
offering a selection of exquisite

PRICE CATEGORIES

For a three-course meal for one with half
a bottle of wine (or equivalent meal),
taxes and extra charges.

D Under AED 100 **DD** AED 100–400
DDD Over AED 400

dishes served in wholesome
portions, alongside a signature
range of delicious cheesecakes.

6 Fujiya
MAP E2 ■ Millenium Airport
Hotel ■ 04 602 1105 ■ Open noon–
1am daily ■ DD
This is where Dubai's leading
Japanese chefs eat on their days
off work. Come here for a real
taste of Japan.

7 Traiteur
MAP E2 ■ Park Hyatt Hotel,
Dubai Creek Golf Club ■ 04 602 1814
■ Open 6pm–midnight daily & 12:30–
4pm Fri ■ DDD
Enjoy classic European cuisine and
admire the chic, modern decor here.

8 Boardwalk
MAP E2 ■ Dubai Creek Golf
Club ■ 04 295 6000 ■ Open 8am–
midnight daily ■ DD
Built on a wooden veranda with views
of the creek, this place has a varied
menu featuring light Mediterranean
fare and Eastern-inspired dishes.

9 Anise
MAP E3 ■ InterContinental,
Dubai Festival City ■ 04 701 1131
■ Open 6:30–11:30pm daily ■ DD
Enjoy international fare after some
shopping at Dubai Festival City Mall.

10 Nomad
MAP E2 ■ Jumeirah Creekside
Hotel, Garhoud ■ 04 230 8458 ■ Open
6:30am–midnight daily ■ DD
This one-of-a-kind restaurant
offers a unique experience with
international cuisine and a
vibrant decor.

See map on p58

TOP 10 Bur Dubai

This bustling part of the city is packed with hotels, office blocks and residential developments, yet a century ago it was a sandy area filled with *barasti* (palm frond houses) and windtower houses around the creek. To get a sense of old Bur Dubai visit the historical Al Fahidi neighbourhood (formerly Al Bastakiya), where the charming courtyard houses have been restored beside the creek. This atmospheric district is a quiet oasis amidst the city's hustle and bustle. Here too is the Al Fahidi Fort, now the Dubai Museum. The Shindagha heritage area, right at the creek mouth, is where Dubai's role as an enterprising and cosmopolitan trading city really began. The souks of Bur Dubai are evidence of this.

Panel detail, Architecture Museum

BUR DUBAI

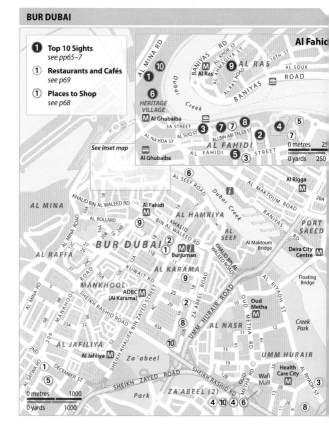

1 Top 10 Sights
see pp65–7

1 Restaurants and Cafés
see p69

1 Places to Shop
see p68

Crossroads of Civilization Museum

MAP J1 ■ Al Khaleej Road ■ 04 393 4440 ■ Open 8am–8pm Sat–Thu ■ Adm ■ www.themuseum.ae

Travel through past ages at this intimate museum. The interesting displays here showcase a world-class array of largely Middle Eastern artifacts, which range from ancient Mesopotamia all the way through to the Ottoman era. Highlights include Egyptian mummy masks, priceless Sumerian sculptures and a beautiful section of *kiswa* (cloth used to drape the Kaaba in the Grand Mosque at Mecca), which was donated by legendary Ottoman ruler Suleiman the Magnificent in 1543.

Dubai Museum and Al Fahidi Fort

Once Dubai's main defence outpost, the imposing sand-coloured Al Fahidi Fort was built in 1788 and has also served as a jail and the ruler's residence. Renovated in 1970, it is now the city museum and worth a look for an informative overview of the Emirates' history. It makes for an entertaining visit for all ages: you can walk through a souk from the 1950s, visit an oasis with a *falaj* (irrigation channel), learn about the desert at night and visit a traditional *barasti* (see pp14–15).

Iranian Mosque

MAP J1

Tucked away in a backstreet off the Textile Souk *(see p66)*, this superb Iranian Mosque (no entrance to non-Muslims) is tricky

Door at the Iranian Mosque

to find but well worth the effort. Following the traditional Persian style, every inch of the building's façade and dome is covered in rich *girih*-style tilework glazed with swathes of deep-blue patterns and embellished with delicate arabesques and swirling floral motifs picked out in yellow and green.

Ruler's Court (Diwan)

MAP K2 ■ Adjacent to Al Fahidi, Creekside

A cream building with imposing wind-towers sits beside the Creek next to the Grand Mosque. The striking gold-topped wrought-iron gates give a clue to its importance: it is the seat of power and the Ruler's Court or *Diwan*, (Persian for couch). Dubai's ruler Sheikh Mohammed's offices are here.

Ruler's Court (Diwan) beside the Creek

5 Al Fahidi

This is one of the oldest and most atmospheric heritage areas in Dubai (see pp18–19). Here you can wander the alleyways between original, restored courtyard houses. Many are crowned with tall windtowers, which were the earliest forms of air conditioning. Late afternoon is the best time to spend a couple of hours here, when the light throws the architecture into golden relief. The area has become a cultural hub, with many buildings converted to art galleries and courtyard cafés.

6 Al Shindagha Museum

MAP J1 ▪ Al Fahidi ▪ 800 33222 ▪ Open 10am–8pm daily

Set along the historic waters of Dubai Creek, Al Shindagha Museum tells the proud story of the nation's past. Highlights of the museum include Perfume House, dedicated to the regional traditions surrounding oud and the intriguing role of fragrance in Arabian society. Now extended, the original building at the core of the complex dates back to 1896 when it was used as the seat of the ruler of Dubai.

Beautiful carpets at the Textile Souk

7 Textile Souk

At the heart of Bur Dubai, the Textile Souk (see p27) begins at the water's edge by the Dubai Old Souk Abra Station. Since the souk's renovation, it is now housed under an imposing arcaded wooden roof, keeping it cool even during the most consuming heat. It's a mix of old and new – here you'll find moneychangers, textiles, bargain clothes, Arabian slippers and curios. The souk (sometimes referred to as the "Old Souk") is great fun to explore – look out for the tailors working on old-fashioned sewing machines. Lanes off the main drag are dotted with examples of local traditional architecture, including long wooden balconies, latticed windows and the occasional windtower.

Inside the Al Shindagha Museum

Hindi Lane
MAP K1

Buried away at the back of the Textile Souk, this delightful "Hindi Lane" (as it is known locally) is one of Dubai's best-hidden secrets. Walking into this narrow lane is like stepping into India itself, with its colourful shops selling religious posters, garlands of flowers and bindis, and other subcontinental paraphernalia. There is even a tiny Sikh temple right above the shops.

 Traditional Architecture Museum
MAP J1 ▪ Al Shindagha waterfront ▪ Open 8am–2pm Sun–Thu ▪ 04 353 1862 ▪ www.dubaiculture.gov.ae

Housed in the beautiful old mansion of Sheikh Juma bin Maktoum, this excellent museum has absorbing displays on the architecture of Dubai and the UAE. Displays cover the different building materials used – stone, mud, coral stone and gypsum – and traditional construction techniques. The museum also houses a variety of traditional tools and ornamentation items used in the construction of houses in Dubai and the Emirates in general.

 Coffee Museum
MAP J1 ▪ Al Fahidi ▪ 04 353 8777 ▪ Open 9am–5pm Sat–Thu ▪ Adm

This fascinating museum dedicated to Arabia's favourite drink spans two floors filled with coffee-related artifacts and accessories. Upstairs there's a coffee bar offering a wide range of superior brews, while downstairs is a gift shop, serving coffee ice-pops, the perfect pick-me-up on a hot summer's day.

MAKTOUM FAMILY'S SETTLEMENT ON DUBAI CREEK

The Maktoum family's reign as rulers of Dubai began in 1833, when Sheikh Maktoum bin Buti and around 800 tribesmen broke away from the Bani Yas tribe of Abu Dhabi. They settled in Shindagha, an ideal location for trade and for the development of Dubai's pearling and fishing industries.

A DAY'S EXPLORATION OF OLD DUBAI

 MORNING

Start your tour at **Al Fahidi Fort**, where you can experience this remarkable heritage neighbourhood. Enjoy a fresh lemon and mint juice at any of the nearby waterside restaurants, or visit the **Coffee Museum** for a taste of Arabia's favourite hot drink – or even a coffee-flavoured ice-pop.

Afterwards, head north up Dubai Creek to **Al Shindagha Museum** to learn about the development of the creek and the history of Arabian perfumes. Following the curve of the creek back towards **Dubai Museum**, you will arrive at the wooden-arcaded **Textile Souk**. Browse the textile stalls and hole-in-the-wall restaurants here. Also peep down the alleyways for views of restored barasti wind towers. By the water, you'll see the abra (water taxi) station. Hop on board for AED 1 rides across the water or take a boat tour. The boat rides offer stunning views of the city's skyline.

AFTERNOON

Head along Al-Fahidi St to the Al Fahidi area where you can enjoy a leisurely courtyard lunch inside the restored building of the **Arabian Tea House Café** *(see pp18–19)*. Afterwards, spend some time exploring Al Fahidi's alleys and buildings; don't miss traditional middle-eastern cuisine at **Bastakiah Nights Restaurant** *(see p19)* and the bijou **Majlis Gallery** *(see p38)*.

See map on p64 ←

Places to Shop

Burjuman Mall, spread out over several stylish levels

1 Burjuman Mall
MAP J3 ▪ Trade Centre Rd ▪ 04 352 0222 ▪ Open 10am–11pm daily

This chic shopping mall features high-end stores selling exclusive labels and glam accessories.

2 Jashanmal "Around the World"
MAP J3 ▪ Burjuman Mall ▪ 04 325 4698 ▪ Open 10am–10pm daily (until 11pm Thu & Fri)

Offering accessories, suitcases and bags from multiple brands, this is the best store for travel essentials.

3 Meena Bazaar
MAP J2 ▪ Near Al Fahidi St, Bur Dubai ▪ Open 9am–10pm daily

A network of streets in Bur Dubai, crammed with shops selling a host of intriguing articles such as handcrafted textiles and jewellery, and traditional handicrafts. There are also several Indian restaurants and cafés here.

4 Wafi Gourmet
MAP H5 ▪ Wafi City ▪ 04 324 4433 ▪ Open 10am–10pm daily (until midnight Thu & Fri)

Stocked with Arabian cheeses and sweets, barrels of olives and dates, plus boxes of Lebanese delights, this is Dubai's favourite delicatessen.

5 Satwa
MAP E2

This suburb is known for its fabrics, tailors and Indian sweet shops. It is where the local people go to shop.

6 Wafi City
MAP E2 ▪ Oud Metha Rd ▪ 04 324 4555 ▪ Open 10am–10pm daily (until midnight Thu & Fri)

This kitsch, Egyptian-themed, pyramid-shaped building is the very best place to head if you love fashion.

7 Textile Souk
Wander through this old renovated souk (see p66) with small shops and stalls selling a medley of goods, from textiles and shoes to bargain clothing and curios.

8 Karama Souk
Hunt for cheap Arabian souvenirs, handicrafts and designer-inspired goods at this shopping complex (see p27). For a sense of local life, wander around the neighbourhood afterwards.

9 Computer Plaza
MAP F7 ▪ Al-Ain Centre ▪ 04 261 2443 ▪ Open 10am–10pm daily

This shopping centre, with over 60 specialized retail outlets, is the perfect place to pick up a discounted laptop or digital camera. A range of software is also available.

10 Ajmal
MAP J3 ▪ Burjuman Mall ▪ 04 351 5505 ▪ Open 10am–10pm daily (until 11pm Thu & Fri)

Specializing in Arabic perfumes, which are stronger and spicier than Western fragrances, this store will mix you a signature scent.

Restaurants and Cafés

1 **Ravi**
MAP E4 ▪ Satwa Roundabout
▪ 04 331 5353 ▪ Open 5am–3am
daily ▪ No alcohol ▪ D

With its famed butter chicken, Ravi is something of an institution. An inexpensive local favourite, this place serves great Pakistani cuisine. The tables here are always packed.

2 **Calicut Paragon**
MAP J4 ▪ Opposite Lulu Centre, Al Karama ▪ 04 335 8700
▪ Open 7am–12:30am daily ▪ D

Savour the coastal cuisine of Calicut, Kerala, at this restaurant. Be sure to try the exceptional seafood curries prepared with aromatic spices.

3 **Awtar**
MAP E2 ▪ Grand Hyatt ▪ 04 317 2221 ▪ Open 7:30pm–3am Tue–Sun ▪ DD

With interiors styled like an opulent tent, Awtar is designed to conjure the impression of dining as a guest of Arabian royalty. Expect Arabian songs and belly dancing at this iconic grotto.

4 **Khan Murjan**
MAP E2 ▪ Souk Khan Murjan, Wafi ▪ 04 327 9795 ▪ Open 9am–12:30am daily ▪ DD

A lovely courtyard restaurant that locals flock to for fantastic Arabian food. Dishes range from Lebanese staples to Egyptian, Moroccan and Iranian classics, alongside some traditional Gulf dishes.

5 **Bastakiah Nights**
With its rooftop offering unrivalled views of old Dubai, this restaurant *(see p19)* is a must-visit for traditional Arabic and Emirati cuisine.

6 **Al Fanar**
MAP K2 ▪ Al Seef ▪ 04 396 6669 ▪ Open 10:30am–11pm daily ▪ DD

Atmospheric Al Fanar features recipes passed down by the founder's grandmother.

PRICE CATEGORIES

For a three-course meal for one with half a bottle of wine (or equivalent meal), taxes and other charges.

D Under AED 100 **DD** AED 100–400
DDD Over AED 400

---

7 **Arabian Tea House Café**
MAP K2 ▪ 04 353 5071 ▪ Open 8am–11pm daily

For a sense of Arabia, enjoy lunch at this alcohol-free, bougainvillea-clad café *(see p19)* in a historic courtyard.

8 **Peppercrab**
MAP E2 ▪ Grand Hyatt Dubai
▪ 04 317 2221 ▪ Open 7–11:30pm daily (until midnight Fri & Sat) ▪ DDD

Devour a tasty, peppery crab at this Singaporean seafood restaurant (aprons and pliers are provided).

9 **Eric's**
MAP J3 ▪ 10 B St, Sheikh Hamdan Colony, Al Karama ▪ 04 396 5080 ▪ Opening hours vary; call ahead ▪ D

The wide range of traditional dishes offered at this delightful restaurant have wholesome Goan flavours.

10 **Asha's**
MAP E2 ▪ Pyramids Wafi City
▪ 04 324 4100 ▪ Open 12:30–3pm & 7:30pm–midnight daily ▪ DDD

Owned by celebrated Bollywood singer Asha Bhosle, this place is known for Indian classics and daring creations.

Asha's eye-catching interior

See map on p64

TOP 10 Sheikh Zayed Road and Downtown Dubai

Dubai's key artery, Sheikh Zayed Road, is a defining symbol of the city's meteoric development, flanked with a giddying array of soaring skyscrapers of every imaginable shape and size. Even Sheikh Zayed Road's futuristic skyline, however, is eclipsed by the record-breaking Downtown Dubai development just to the south. Here you'll find some of the city's most ambitious modern mega-developments, including the world's largest mall, its biggest fountain, and Burj Khalifa, the tallest building on the planet.

The gleaming Emirates Tower

1 Emirates Towers
MAP D6 ▪ Sheikh Zayed Rd
▪ 04 330 0000

Two triangular twin towers, the Jumeirah Emirates Towers clad in aluminium and silver glass, soar into Sheikh Zayed Road's skyline. The taller one serves as an office block, where Dubai ruler Sheikh Mohammed bin Rashid Al Maktoum has his office, while the other is home to a 400-bedroom luxury hotel joined by a central podium containing a shopping boulevard. The hotel and boulevard have a great choice of restaurants and bars. Shopping options include international fashion from top designers, jewellery and antiques.

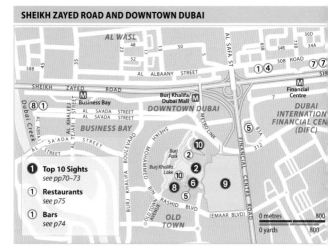

SHEIKH ZAYED ROAD AND DOWNTOWN DUBAI

1 **Top 10 Sights**
see pp70–73

1 **Restaurants**
see p75

1 **Bars**
see p74

Dubai Fountain puts on a display

③ Dubai World Trade Centre

MAP E5 ■ Sheikh Zayed Rd ■ 04 332 1000 ■ www.dwtc.com

Although dwarfed today by the skyscrapers of Sheikh Zayed Rd, the DWTC was the tallest building in the city back in 1979, and was opened with great pomp by Sheikh Rashid and Queen Elizabeth II of England. It has played an important role in the city's development, a fact reflected by the continued use of its image on the AED 100 note. Today, the centre also comprises 14 huge exhibition halls. The Dubai International Convention Centre next door can accommodate more than 10,000.

② Dubai Fountain

MAP C6 ■ Displays every 30 min 6–11pm daily (also 1pm & 1:30pm Sat–Thu)

Filling the space between the Burj Khalifa, Dubai Mall and Souk al Bahar is the spectacular Dubai Fountain, the world's largest. It features an extraordinary array of jets illuminated with 6,000 lights which fire plumes of water 150 m (492 ft) into the air. Located in the middle of a lake, the fountain puts on an amazing show after dusk when colourful sprays of water erupt dancing in time to an accompanying musical soundtrack.

④ DIFC and the Gate

MAP D6 ■ Sheikh Zayed Rd ■ 04 362 2222

Behind Emirates Towers is the Gate, the striking 15-storey architectural signature of the Dubai International Financial Centre (DIFC). This "city within a city" now serves as a global financial hub with its own civil and commercial laws. The Gate is shaped like a bridge – DIFC is designed to bridge the gap between the financial centres of London and New York in the West and Hong Kong and Tokyo in the East. The attached Gate Village is stuffed with upmarket galleries.

DIFC and the Gate

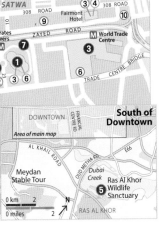

Flamingos at Ras Al Khor Sanctuary

boutiques, souvenir shops and antique stores. Along the souk's pleasant waterfront promenade there are several restaurants, cafés and lounge bars. This is the perfect spot for a stroll before you attempt the shopping madness of the Dubai Mall, which is just a few minutes' walk away.

⑤ Ras Al Khor Wildlife Sanctuary

MAP E2 ■ Ras Al Khor ■ 800 900 ■ Open 9am–4pm Sat–Thu ■ Free entry to the hides; groups of more than 10 require permits

Pink flamingos, waders and other birds can be viewed on a marshy reserve at the inner end of Dubai Creek. This urban reserve has two hides: Flamingo and Mangrove. Both are fitted out with telescopes, binoculars and picture panels.

⑥ Souk Al Bahar

MAP C6 ■ Sheikh Mohammed bin Rashid Blvd ■ 04 362 7011 ■ Open 10am–10pm Sat–Thu, 2–10pm Fri ■ www.soukalbahar.ae

Next to the futuristic Burj Khalifa is a slice of old, albeit newly built, Arabia. Souk Al Bahar is an Arabesque shopping mall with over 100 retail outlets including independent

Exterior of The Palace Hotel

⑦ Museum of the Future

MAP D6 ■ Sheikh Zayed Rd ■ Open 10am–7:30pm daily ■ Adm ■ www.museumofthefuture.ae

This remarkable museum is an initiative of the Dubai Future Foundation, which sets out to explore the most pressing issues relating to humanity's collective future. Housed in a beautiful silver orb, the museum uses cutting-edge technologies to explore climate change, the future of artificial intelligence and new forms of social organization.

⑧ Palace Downtown

MAP C6 ■ Downtown Burj Khalifa ■ 04 428 7888 ■ www.theaddress.com

Tucked away behind Souk al Bahar is the opulent Palace Downtown. The hotel's exquisite Arabian-style façade and palm-lined ornamental pool are sights in their own right, made all the more memorable by the hotel's incongruous juxtaposition with the futuristic Burj Khalifa *(see pp12–13)* rising directly behind. The hotel's Thiptara restaurant *(see p75)* offers fine Thai dining and peerless views of the Dubai Fountain.

⑨ The Dubai Mall

MAP C6 ■ Next to the Burj Khalifa ■ Open 10am–10pm Sun–Wed, 10am–midnight Thu–Sat ■ www.thedubaimall.com

The ultimate shrine to consumerism, this mall has a vast array of shops and other attractions, including the Dubai Aquarium, an ice rink and a skeleton of a 150-million-year-old diplodocus dinosaur. Highlights include the Arabian-themed souk section and the ultra-chic Fashion Avenue. The selection of places to eat include some nice alfresco places overlooking the Dubai Fountain.

The Dubai Mall, a retail heaven

⑩ Burj Khalifa

Named after the UAE president Sheikh Khalifa bin Zayed Al Nahyan, the Burj Khalifa (see pp12–13) is far and away the tallest man-made structure on the planet. Most of the tower is residential but a pair of observation decks are open to visitors and the base of the building houses the world's first Armani Hotel.

GODOLPHIN

The famous Godolphin racing stable was established by the equestrian-loving Maktoum Royal Family of Dubai in 1994. It has won Group One races in 11 countries. It bred the great Dubai Millennium, who won the Dubai World Cup 2000 by over six lengths and sired 59 offspring (see www.godolphin.com).

A STROLL AMONGST THE SKYSCRAPERS

Sheikh Zayed Road · Burj Khalifa Lake · Burj Khalifa · Noodle House · Emirates Towers · Dubai Fountain · The Dubai Mall · The Palace Hotel · The Address Downtown · Souk Al Bahar, Karma Kafé

▶ MORNING

Begin the morning with a stroll down **Sheikh Zayed Road** (see pp12–13), starting at the **Emirates Towers** (see p70) and admiring the area's many super-tall skyscrapers. **Noodle House** (see p75), about halfway down the strip, is a great place to grab a delicious noodle bowl to snack on. Head on to **The Dubai Mall** and spend time exploring the shops here. If shopping doesn't appeal, there are plenty of other attractions at the mall, including the Dubai Aquarium or the chance to go for a cooling spin at the ice rink. Lunch can be found in one of the mall's cafés.

AFTERNOON

After lunch head to the pretty, Arabian-themed **Souk Al Bahar**, where more shops await. Then pop into **The Palace Hotel** for tea before making a late afternoon visit to the observation deck of the **Burj Khalifa** for Dubai's most amazing views (reserve tickets in advance).

As dusk begins to fall, go out onto the promenade surrounding **Burj Khalifa Lake** (see p12) and watch the show-stopping **Dubai Fountain** spring into life. Next, head to **The Address Downtown** (see pp12–13) and enjoy a snack at the sophisticated lobby lounge that offers gourmet sandwiches, scones and handpicked signature blends. Alternatively, head to the pan-Asian **Karma Kafé** (see p75) in Souk Al Bahar or to one of the many waterside restaurants to end your Downtown Dubai day with dinner.

See map on pp70–71

Bars

1 Weslodge
MAP A6 ▪ JW Marriott Marquis, Business Bay ▪ 054 509 3025 ▪ Open 5:30pm–2am daily ▪ www.weslodge.ae

A stylish, rock-and-roll-themed bar (see p47), known for its creative drinks and superb North American cuisine.

2 The Bar at Avli by Tashas
MAP D6 ▪ Unit C-01, Ground Floor, Gate Village Building 9 ▪ 04 359 0008 ▪ Open 7pm–1am Sun–Wed ▪ www.avlibytashas.com

A key feature of this gorgeous Greek restaurant is its central bar.

3 Cin Cin
MAP E5 ▪ Fairmont Hotel ▪ 04 311 8316 ▪ Open 7pm–3am daily ▪ www.fairmont.com

This chic champagne bar has a great snack menu with freshly-shucked oysters and Wagyu beefburgers.

4 The Balcony Bar
MAP C5 ▪ Shangri-La Hotel ▪ 04 405 2703 ▪ Open 9am–3am daily

An ideal place to unwind, this swanky restaurant overlooks the hotel's lobby. Enjoy drinks while soaking up the ambience.

A seafood dish on the menu at Vault

5 Galaxy Bar
MAP D6 ▪ Unit C-01, Ground Floor, Gate Village Building 9 ▪ Open 8pm–3am Sun–Thu

Ranked 45 on the World's 50 Best Bars in 2022, this glamorous bar (see p46) serves excellent cocktails in the heart of fashionable DIFC.

6 Blue Bar
MAP E5 ▪ Novotel World Trade Centre ▪ 04 332 0000 ▪ Open noon–2am daily

A low-key relaxed bar where you can chill to the tunes of the resident band.

Colonial-style interior at Long's Bar

7 Long's Bar
MAP D5 ▪ Towers Rotana Hotel ▪ 04 312 2202 ▪ Open noon–3am daily ▪ www.rotana.com

This colonial-style bar, with its small dance floor, claims to have the longest bar in the whole of the UAE.

8 Vault
MAP B6 ▪ Business Bay ▪ 0414 6339 ▪ Open 5pm–3am daily ▪ www.jwmarriottmarquis dubailife.com

One of the world's highest bars, Vault (see p46) is located on the 72nd floor of the JW Marriott Marquis hotel. Svelte decor and classy ambience complement the panoramic views.

9 Fibber McGees
MAP D5 ▪ Off Sheikh Zayed Rd ▪ 04 332 2400 ▪ Open 8am–2am daily ▪ www.fibbersdubai.com

Dubai's best traditional pub is tricky to find (check directions on the website) but worth the effort. The homely interior transports you straight to Ireland, as do the draught Kilkenny and Guinness. There's good food, too, plus regular live music.

10 Miss Lily's
MAP E5 ▪ Sheraton Grand Hotel ▪ Open 7pm–2am daily ▪ 04 356 2900 ▪ www.misslilys.com

A charming Caribbean bar with delightful house cocktails and spirits. The flavourful dishes served here draw from distinct Jamaican roots.

Restaurants

Hoi An
MAP C5 ■ Shangri-La Hotel, Sheikh Zayed Rd ■ 04 405 2703 ■ Open 7pm–midnight daily & 12:30–4pm Fri & Sat ■ DDD

Vietnamese fare served in elegant surroundings (see p47) with a range of dishes and excellent service.

At.Mosphere
MAP C6 ■ 122nd Floor, Burj Khalifa ■ 04 888 3828 ■ Opening hours vary; call ahead ■ DDD

This place (see p47) offers exceptional European-style fine dining on the 122nd floor of the Burj Khalifa.

Avli by Tashas
MAP D6 ■ Unit C-01, Ground Floor, Gate Village Building 9 ■ 04 359 0008 ■ Open noon–4pm & 7pm–1am Sun–Wed ■ DDD

Dubai's most fashionable Greek restaurant, this is the best place to enjoy fine dining.

Exchange Grill
MAP E5 ■ Fairmont Hotel ■ 04 332 5555 ■ Open 7pm–midnight daily ■ DDD

This steakhouse serves delicious melt-in-the mouth Kobo steak.

Karma Kafé
MAP C6 ■ Souk Al Bahar, Downtown Burj Khalifa ■ 04 423 8306 ■ Open 3pm–1am daily ■ DD

Enjoy classic Asian fusion food in the plush interior or on the lovely terrace

---

of this upscale Pan-Asian restaurant. The views of the nearby Burj Khalifa and Dubai Fountain are magnificent.

Ninive
MAP E6 ■ Emirates Towers Bd ■ 04 326 6105 ■ Open Open 6pm–2am Sun–Thu (to 3am Fri & Sat ■ DD

One of the best Arabian restaurants, it offers delectable mezze, grills and seafood in an open-air setting.

Teatro
MAP D5 ■ Towers Rotana Hotel ■ 04 312 2202 ■ Open 6pm–2am daily ■ DD

The great cross-Continental dishes here have made this restaurant a firm favourite for many years.

The Noodle House
MAP D6 ■ Dubai International Financial Centre ■ 04 363 7093 ■ Open noon–10:30pm daily ■ DD

Visit this place for a quick, affordable and very tasty bowl of spicy noodles.

Le Petit Maison
MAP D6 ■ Dubai International Financial Centre ■ 04 439 0505 ■ Open 7–11am, noon–3pm, 7–11pm daily ■ DD

Reminiscent of the Côte d'Azur, this place has a delightful menu of French Mediterranean and Niçoise cuisine.

Thiptara
MAP C6 ■ The Palace Hotel ■ 04 428 7888 ■ Open 6–11:30pm Sat–Thu, 12:30–4pm & 6–11:30pm Fri ■ DDD

Set in a beautiful wooden pavilion on the lakeside, this venue specializes in Thai seafood. Book ahead.

Elegant decor in the Karma Kafé

See map on pp70–71

🔟 Jumeirah

Stretching down the coast southwest from the port area, Jumeirah is one of the most glamorous and sought-after of all the city suburbs. It's no surprise that residential property here is pricey – it's the ultimate location for a place in the sun and the quiet leafy streets are filled with bougainvillea-clad luxury villas. At the southern end of the district the extensive low-rise suburbs are punctuated by three of the city's most famous landmarks: the iconic "seven-star" Burj Al Arab Jumeirah, the enormous wave-shaped Jumeirah Beach Hotel and the vast mock-Arabian Madinat Jumeirah complex (home to the beautiful Souk Madinat Jumeirah). Staying here is an expensive pleasure, but the area's beaches, bars and restaurants are amongst the finest in the city, while the Wild Wadi Water Park offers watery thrills and spills for those energetic enough to leave the beach.

The Burj Al Arab Jumeirah

1 Burj Al Arab Jumeirah

Visible from almost anywhere in Jumeirah, the Burj Al Arab Jumeirah (see p113), a stunning luxury hotel, is a symbol of the city itself and is distinguished by its unusual shape mirroring the billowing sail of a *dhow*. Advance reservations are needed to visit the interior of this opulent hotel (see pp24–5). For a great close-up view of the exterior, drop into the Jumeirah Beach Hotel and take the super-fast glass elevator to the top floor.

JUMEIRAH

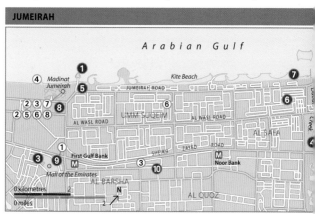

Jumeirah Mosque, a fine example of modern Islamic architecture

2 Jumeirah Mosque

Rising proudly above Jumeirah Road, the imposing Fatimid-style Jumeirah Mosque (see pp20–21) is one of the city's most impressive and attractive mosques.

3 Ski Dubai Snow Park

MAP C2 ■ Mall of the Emirates ■ 600 599905 ■ Open 10am–midnight Sun–Thu, 9am–midnight Fri & Sat ■ Adm ■ www.skidxb.com

You can't miss Ski Dubai (see p44) from the Sheikh Zayed Road, jutting out like a giant space-age tube.

Filled with over 6,000 tonnes of snow, it offers five slopes, linked by chair-lifts and tow lifts, to cater to all ski levels, including the longest black indoor run in the world. There's also a snow park for little ones, plus a set of thrilling rides and activities such as snowboarding.

4 Safa Park

MAP A5

A ride on the giant Ferris wheel here offers the best views of this land-scaped green park stretching from Al Wasl Road to Sheikh Zayed Road, now cut through by the meandering Dubai Water Canal, an extension of Dubai Creek. It is hugely popular with local residents, many of whom make the most of its specially-sprung perimeter jogging track. It's great for kids to run free and there's lots of entertainment, including a mini-train, a merry-go-round and a lake with rowing boats.

Top 10 Sights
see pp76–9

Restaurants and Bars
see p81

Places to Shop
see p80

Verdant and leafy Safa Park

Attractions at Wild Wadi Water Park

5 Wild Wadi Water Park
MAP C2 ■ Jumeirah Rd
■ 04 348 4444 ■ Opening hours vary; check website for timings
■ Adm ■ www.wildwadi.com
■ Cashless payment system using electronic waterproof wristband

This world-class water park offers a great day out to suit all ages and bravery levels with 30 water-fuelled rides and attractions. Thrill-seekers will not be disappointed by its most challenging ride, Jumeirah Sceirah, the tallest and fastest freefall water slide outside the US. Well-staffed by lifeguards and with plenty of food outlets, it makes for a fun day out.

JUMEIRAH'S BEACHES AND DUBAI'S BEACH CULTURE

All of the hotels in Jumeirah are fronted by their own private stretches of golden beach onto the Arabian Gulf, but there are plenty of public beaches too, which fill up at weekends. There are also family-friendly beach parks with a small entrance charge: the best in this area is the Jumeirah Beach Park.

6 Majlis Ghorfat um al Sheef
MAP D2 ■ 17 St ■ 800 33222
■ Open 8:30am–10:30pm Sun–Thu, 3–10pm Fri & Sat ■ Adm

Hidden amongst the suburban sprawl the Majlis Ghorfat um al Sheef is the only historic building to survive outside the old city centre. Built in 1955, this quaint two-storey structure served as a summer retreat for visionary former ruler Sheikh Rashid, with sleeping quarters below and a *majlis* (meeting room) above. The garden has date palm trees watered using traditional *falaj* irrigation channels.

7 Jumeirah Beach Park
MAP A4

This lovely green park, backs onto a beautiful white-sand beach. You can access the beach from the park along wooden walkways and there is plenty of shade on the sand under the palm trees. It's equipped with lifeguards, and has good facilities. Some small cafés are also lined along the beach.

Shoreline at Jumeirah Beach Park

8 Madinat Jumeirah

MAP C2 ■ Al Sufouh Rd

This vast leisure and entertainment complex is a major focus of the Jumeirah area. It has three hotels linked by waterways navigated by silent battery-powered *abras*. There are numerous restaurants, bars and cafés, many with great waterside views, with the seafood restaurant Pierchic *(see p81)* located on a pier that stretches into the Arabian Gulf. Also located here is the Souk Madinat Jumeirah *(see p80)*, a reconstruction of a traditional Arabian bazaar.

Abras at Madinat Jumeirah

9 Mall of the Emirates

MAP C2 ■ Interchange 4
■ 800 663 6255 ■ www.mallofthe emirates.com

Dubai's swankiest retail complex has more than 500 shops, selling every product you can possibly dream of. There's also a Harvey Nichols and Debenhams. Other attractions include a multi-screen cinema and kids' play area Magic Planet *(see p44)*, plus dozens of cafés and restaurants.

10 Al Quoz Galleries

MAP C2 ■ www.alserkal avenue.ae

The gritty industrial area of Al Quoz has been transformed by the cutting-edge art galleries that have moved into the area. Many local galleries are relocating into the Alserkal Avenue arts centre on Street 8, including leading names like Efie Gallery and Green Art Gallery *(see p38)*.

A DAY BY THE SEA

▶ MORNING

Start your day with breakfast on the outdoor terrace of **Lime Tree Café** *(see p81)*. Enjoy the gentle morning sun as you sip on some coffee or a juice. Then take an insightful morning tour of the **Jumeirah Mosque** *(see pp20–21)* for the chance to look inside one of Dubai's finest Islamic buildings. Drive or hire a taxi to **Jumeirah Beach Park**, where you can swim or laze under the palm trees.

AFTERNOON

Leave at lunchtime and head to **Madinat Jumeirah**, where you can enjoy a leisurely late lunch at a huge choice of restaurants, many overlooking the waterways. Afterwards spend an hour or two window-shopping for souvenirs or browsing the lovely Arabian-style **Souk Madinat Jumeirah** *(see p80)* here.

As evening approaches, head to one of Dubai's most beautiful bars, the **Bahri Bar** *(see p81)* housed in the luxurious Mina A'Salam hotel *(see p113)*. From this beautiful alfresco spot, you can sip a cocktail whilst enjoying superb views of the **Burj Al Arab Jumeirah** *(see pp24–5)* and watching the sun set over the Gulf. There are numerous places to eat dinner nearby, but for pure romance head to the delectable **Pai Thai** *(see p81)* in the nearby **Dar al Masyaf** hotel. With fine Thai cuisine in a magical setting which overlooks the meandering waterways of the Medinat and the Burj, a meal here is hard to beat. It is recommended to ● book in advance.

See map on pp76–7

Places to Shop

1 Mall of the Emirates
Prepare to shop until you drop at one of the biggest shopping centres (see p79) in the region.

2 Camel Company
MAP C2 ■ Souk Madinat Jumeirah ■ 04 368 6048 ■ Open 10am–11pm daily ■ www.camelcompany.ae
Dubai's cutest selection of cuddly toy camels and other dromedary-themed souvenirs – perfect for kids.

3 Times Square Center
MAP C2 ■ Sheikh Zayed Rd ■ 04 341 8020 ■ Open 10am–10pm daily (until midnight Fri & Sat) ■ www.timessquarecenter.ae
This mall features an impressive electronics store. It also has an ice lounge where everything, from the tables to the glasses, is made of ice.

4 The Village Mall
MAP D4 ■ Jumeirah Rd ■ 04 344 9514 ■ Open 10am–10pm Sat–Thu, 2–10pm Fri
An intriguing mix of niche upmarket boutiques fill this pretty shopping centre, with its archways, plants and fountains. It is the perfect place to find a one-of-a-kind gift.

5 Souk Madinat Jumeirah
MAP C2 ■ Al Sufouh Rd ■ Open 10am–11pm daily
This magical bazaar has art, jewellery, antiques and handicrafts, interspersed with great bars and restaurants.

Souk Madinat Jumeirah

6 Pride of Kashmir
MAP C2 ■ Souk Madinat Jumeirah ■ 04 368 6110 ■ Open 10am–11pm daily ■ www.prideofkashmir.com
A craft and souvenir shop packed with antique and modern rugs from Iran, Kashmir and Turkey.

7 Boxpark
MAP D2 ■ Al Wasl Rd ■ 800 637227 ■ Open 10am–10pm daily (until midnight Thu–Sat) ■ www.boxpark.ae
A funky retail space made up of minimalist cuboid buildings with the odd shipping container poking out, housing eclectic and offbeat shops.

8 Gallery One
MAP C2 ■ Souk Madinat Jumeirah ■ 04 368 6055 ■ Open 10am–11pm daily ■ www.g-1.com
This commercial gallery specializes in selling beautiful but relatively affordable limited-edition Arabian- and Asian-themed artworks.

9 Mercato Mall
MAP C4 ■ Jumeirah Beach Rd ■ 04 344 4161 ■ Open 10am–10pm daily ■ ww.mercatoshoppingmall.com
An Italian-themed mall with 90 shops, restaurants and cafés. With a fun soft play area, it is great for kids.

10 Jumeirah Plaza
MAP D4 ■ Jumeirah Rd ■ 04 349 0766 ■ Open 10am–10pm Sat–Thu, 1:30–10pm Fri
This small mall, popular with local residents, has a pleasant coffee shop with an outdoor terrace.

Restaurants and Bars

PRICE CATEGORIES
For a three-course meal for one with half a bottle of wine (or equivalent meal), taxes and extra charges.

D Under AED 100 **DD** AED 100–400 **DDD** Over AED 400

1 COYA Dubai
MAP D4 ■ Four Seasons Resort ■ 04 316 9600 ■ Opening hours vary; call ahead ■ DD

Exquisite Peruvian dishes fused with Japanese, Chinese and Spanish elements are on offer at this venue.

2 Zheng He's
MAP C1 ■ Mina A' Salam, Madinat Jumeirah ■ 800 323 232 ■ Open noon–3pm & 6:30–11:30pm daily ■ DDD

Dine on fresh seafood and Chinese cuisine by the harbourfront.

3 Trattoria
MAP C2 ■ Madinat Jumeirah ■ 800 323 232 ■ Open noon–midnight daily ■ DD

Delicious Italian fare is served in a mock Venetian waterway setting.

4 Pierchic
MAP C1 ■ Al Qasr, Madinat Jumeirah ■ 800 323 232 ■ Open 12:30–3pm Sat–Fri & 6:15pm–midnight Sat & Sun ■ DDD

Book a terrace table at this seafood restaurant on a wooden pier.

5 Lime Tree Café
MAP D4 ■ Jumeirah Rd ■ 04 325 6325 ■ Open 7:30am–5:30pm daily ■ No alcohol ■ D

This homely café with an outdoor terrace serves healthy homemade lunches, soups, juices, tea and coffee.

6 Maria Bonita's Taco Shop
MAP C2 ■ Umm Al Sheif St ■ 04 395 5576 ■ Open noon–midnight daily ■ No alcohol ■ D

Be transported to Mexico with some good-value tacos, tortillas and salsas.

7 Bahri Bar
MAP C2 ■ Mina A' Salam, Madinat Jumeirah ■ 800 323 232 ■ Open 4pm–2am daily ■ DD

With a large terrace and views of the Burj Al Arab Jumeirah light shows, this is an ideal spot for a sundowner.

Elegant surroundings at Bahri Bar

8 Sho Cho's
MAP E4 ■ Dubai Marine Beach Resort & Spa ■ 050 798 1869 ■ Opening hours vary; call ahead ■ DD

This super-chic Japanese bar offers a gorgeous terrace overlooking the Gulf.

9 Nusr-Et Steakhouse
MAP D4 ■ Four Seasons Resort ■ 04 407 4100 ■ Opening hours vary; call ahead ■ DD

A unique restaurant founded by the internet sensation Chef Nusret Gökçe, known popularly as Salt Bae. It celebrates the tradition of Turkish-style steakhouses and has a superb menu.

10 Hoseki
MAP D2 ■ Bulgari Resort, Jumeirah 2 ■ 044 777 5433 ■ Open 1–11pm Wed–Sun ■ DDD

A Michelin-starred restaurant *(see p47)* serving exquisite Japanese food by chef Masahiro Sugiyama. Each dish is specifically catered to the individual diner.

See map on pp76–7

TOP 10 Dubai Marina and Palm Jumeirah

Far south of the city you'll find the most evidence of modern Dubai's growth. Twenty years ago, most of this area was nothing but sand and sea. Now, it's a whole new city within a city. The skyscrapers of the Dubai Marina district run unbroken for several kilometres along the coast, enclosing a futuristic marina that is backed by a swathe of beach and huge resorts. Offshore lies the Palm Jumeirah, the world's largest human-made island, crowned by the Atlantis resort.

Dubai Marina

DUBAI MARINA AND PALM JUMEIRAH

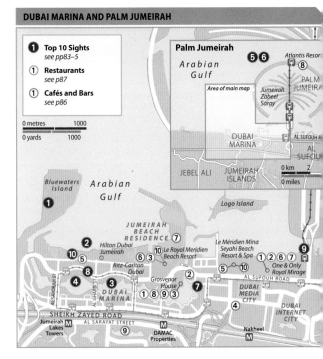

① Top 10 Sights
see pp83–5

① Restaurants
see p87

① Cafés and Bars
see p86

0 metres   1000
0 yards   1000

The Ain Dubai, Bluewaters Island

1 Bluewaters Island
MAP B1

At the end of Jumeirah Beach Residence, connected via a picturesque footbridge, is the Bluewaters Island development, which is home to the Ain Dubai (Dubai Eye), the world's largest Ferris wheel. The wheel offers incredible views over the waterfront, and each capsule is fitted with LCD screens which point out prominent structures on the skyline. On the island, there are also several trendy restaurants and bars including Chinese den Shi and the London Project. Explore the wealth of attractions here, or simply spend the day chilling at Cove Beach Club.

2 Aqua Fun
MAP B1 ■ Jumeirah Beach Residences ■ Open 9am–sunset daily ■ www.aquafun.ae

The world's largest inflatable waterpark, just off the shore of Jumeirah Beach Residence, Aqua Fun is an obstacle course of slippery wet slides and tubes. The challenge is to not slip and fall into the water. It's much harder than it looks and provides great fun for all the family.

3 Boat Trips at the Marina

The marina development is definitely a place best appreciated from the water, and there are a range of boat trips available to make this possible. The cheapest and simplest option is to take a ride on one of the water taxis, which shuttle up and down the marina itself, and there are also after-dark dinner cruises aboard traditional *dhows*. Alternatively, catch a ride on the Dubai Ferry *(see p105)* that runs between Bur Dubai and the marina or go for a sightseeing tour with the Yellow Boats *(see p55)*.

4 Dubai Marina
MAP B2

Centrepiece of the Dubai Marina development is the expansive marina itself, lined with millionaires' boats and surrounded by skyscrapers on all sides. It is particularly impressive when illuminated after dark. Created out of a human-made sea inlet running parallel to the ocean, the marina is the best part of the 3-km- (2-mile-) long shoreline. Disoriented sharks and even whales have been known to swim into it from time to time.

Having fun on an inflatable obstacle course at Aqua Fun

Interior of Atlantis, The Palm

⑤ Atlantis, The Palm

Dominating the far end of the Palm Jumeirah is the vast Atlantis, The Palm resort *(see p113)*. This is one of the city's most distinctive landmarks, a soaring pink colossus arranged around a vast Arabian-style archway. The lavish interior is a riot of gold columns and marble floors. Nearby attractions include Aquaventure and a vast swathe of delightfully golden beach.

⑥ Aquaventure

MAP B1 ▪ Atlantis, The Palm ▪ 04 426 2000 ▪ Open 10am–sunset ▪ Adm ▪ www.atlantisthepalm.com

The Aquaventure water park offers state-of-the-art rides and attractions. The highlight is the huge Leap of Faith water slide, which lands you in a transparent tunnel in a shark-filled lagoon. Guests staying at Atlantis, The Palm and the nearby Atlantis, The Royal both have complimentary access to the thrilling water park. Visitors can purchase tickets to the park through the website.

⑦ Marina Walk

MAP B2

Encircling both sides of Dubai Marina is the pedestrianized Marina Walk. An array of cafés and restaurants line the waterfront here, along with the swanky Marina Mall *(see p50)*. At the northern end of the marina, look out for the unmistakeable 73-storey Cayan Tower with its remarkable twisted shape – the entire building rotates over 90°. Across the road, the new Dubai Harbour development now welcomes gleaming cruise ships, which tower over the super yachts.

People stepping out while enjoying the views from Marina Walk

8 The Walk at JBR
MAP B2

Running along the beachfront is the Walk at JBR, a long boulevard of shops, restaurants, cafés and hotels backed by the huge towers of the Jumeirah Beach Residence, which is one of the city's most relaxed places for an outdoor stroll. Adjacent, the Beach at JBR is amongst Dubai's most attractive recent developments, with a low-rise cluster of shops and restaurants arranged around pretty piazzas and fountains.

The Palm Monorail crossing the Gulf

9 Palm Monorail
MAP B1–2 ■ Open 10am–10pm daily (trains every 20–30 min) ■ Adm ■ www.palm-monorail.com

The only place you really get a proper view of the Palm Jumeirah is from the air. If your budget can't quite stretch to a helicopter ride, the Palm Monorail offers the best overview of the development, running on a raised track across the island and offering great views of the Palm and the skyscrapers of Dubai Marina behind.

10 Marina Beach
MAP B2

One of the marina's top draws is its superb swathe of white sand – the best free beach in the city. The size of the beach means that there's usually plenty of space to lounge on (although it does get busy, particularly on weekends), and there are facilities such as showers and changing rooms, plus loungers for hire. This is also the best place in Dubai to arrange water sports, with a wide selection of activities available, including sailing, kayaking, water-skiing and banana boats.

A DAY ON LAND AND OUT AT SEA

▶ MORNING

Start your day with a pleasant stroll around **Dubai Marina** (see p83). Spend an hour or so exploring the shops in the **Marina Mall** or take a boat trip (see p83). Next, walk over to the nearby **Marina Beach**. Take some time to catch the rays or maybe try your hand at one of the water sports on offer there. Afterwards, explore the shops along **The Walk at JBR** and grab some lunch in one of the many cafés and restaurants.

AFTERNOON

After lunch, catch the Dubai tram to Palm Monorail station and ride the **Palm Monorail** across to **Atlantis, The Palm**, with bird's-eye views of the huge **Palm Jumeirah** along the way. Have a look around the vast Atlantis resort's lavish interior.

EVENING

Hop back on board the monorail and head back to the mainland. From Palm Monorail station continue to the nearby **One&Only Royal Mirage** (see p113). You can spend an enjoyable evening here admiring the hotel's magical Moorish architecture and endless palm trees. Start with a drink at Moroccan-style The Rooftop terrace bar (see p86), followed by dinner at one of the resorts excellent restaurants. The pool-fringed Eauzone (see p87) is particularly romantic, but you will need to book ahead.

See map on p82

Cafés and Bars

1 Mr. Miyagi's
MAP B2 ■ Media One, Dubai Media City ■ Open noon–3am daily ■ www.mrmiyagisdubai.com ■ DD

Drop by this vibrantly decorated, *Karate Kid*-themed venue (see p46) popular for its delectable Asian dishes.

2 Siddharta Lounge by Buddha-Bar
MAP B2 ■ Grosvenor House Dubai, Al Emreef St, Dubai Marina ■ Open 6pm–1am Sun–Thu (to 2am Fri & Sat) ■ www.siddhartalounge.com ■ DD

Siddharta Lounge by Buddha-Bar combines a beautiful boho restaurant with an outdoor terrace bar.

3 Bar 44
MAP B2 ■ Grosvenor House, Dubai Marina ■ 04 317 6000 ■ Open 4pm–2am Fri–Wed, 4pm–3am Thu ■ www.bar44-dubai.com ■ DD

This top-floor swanky bar (see p46) with comfy sofas and a giant balcony offers 44 different types of champagne.

4 The Rooftop
MAP B2 ■ Arabian Court, One& Only Royal Mirage, Al Sufouh ■ 04 399 9999 ■ Open 5pm–1am daily ■ D

Visit this Moroccan-styled bar (see p46) for views over the Arabian Gulf and a relaxed drink under a star-filled sky.

5 ATTIKO High Energy Lounge
MAP B2 ■ W Dubai – Mina Seyahi, Dubai Marina ■ Open 5pm–2am Sun–Thu (to 3am Fri & Sat) ■ www.theattiko.com ■ DDD

Inspired by cosmopolitan Asian nightclubs, ATTIKO enjoys 31st-floor views over the Dubai Harbour development and Palm Jumeirah.

6 Caña by Tamoka
MAP B2 ■ Ritz-Carlton Dubai, JBR The Walk, Dubai Marina ■ Open noon–10pm daily ■ www.tamokadubai.com ■ DD

Located on the beach in front of Tamoka Dubai restaurant, this tiny beach hut bar serves great cocktails.

7 Zero Gravity
MAP B1 ■ Al Sufouh Rd ■ 04 399 0009 ■ Opening hours vary, call ahead ■ www.0-gravity.ae ■ D

This beachfront bar-restaurant is a lovely place to linger over a sundowner.

8 Cloud 22
MAP B1 ■ Atlantis, The Royal, Crescent Rd, Palm Jumeirah ■ Open 10am–dusk daily ■ www.atlantis.com/atlantis-the-royal ■ DDD

Cloud 22 is exclusively open to guests of Atlantis, The Royal and it's worth booking a room just to experience it.

9 Nola
MAP B2 ■ Armada BlueBay Hotel, Cluster P, JLT ■ 04 399 8155 ■ Open 12pm–3am daily ■ www.nola-social.com ■ DD

A New Orleans-inspired bar with a lovely ambience (see p47). Book ahead.

10 Barasti
MAP B2 ■ Le Meridien Mina Seyahi Beach Resort & Marina ■ 04 318 1313 ■ Open 10am–3:30am daily ■ www.barastibeach.com ■ DD

Barasti comes alive on the weekends, when revellers sprawl out across the sand. There is live music most nights.

Charming interiors at The Rooftop

Restaurants

1 Pitfire Pizza
MAP B2 ■ Lake Terrace Tower,
Cluster D ■ 800 7483473 ■ Open
11am–11pm daily ■ DD
Dubai's best pizza restaurant
(see p46) serves an array of
traditional and innovative pizzas.

Atmospheric dining at Tagine

2 Tagine
MAP B2 ■ One&Only Royal
Mirage, Al Sufouh ■ 04 399 9999
■ Open 7–11:30pm Tue–Sun ■ DD
Visit this candlelit restaurant for a
magical Moroccan experience. The
courtyard location adds to its charm.

3 Maya
MAP B2 ■ Le Royal Meridien
Beach Resort ■ 04 316 5550 ■ Open
7pm–1am Sat–Wed, 7pm–2am Thu,
12:30–4pm & 7pm–2am Sun ■ DDD
Experience new-wave Mexican cuisine
in spacious surroundings decorated
with Mayan art and modern sculpture.

4 Amala
MAP B1 ■ Jumeirah Zabeel
Saray, Palm Jumeirah ■ 04 453
0444 ■ Open 1–4pm & 6–11:30pm
daily ■ DD
Enjoy tasty North Indian dishes in a
lavish setting with traditional decor.

5 BiCE
MAP B2 ■ Hilton Dubai
Jumeirah ■ 04 318 2520 ■ Open
12:30–3:30pm & 7–11:30pm ■ DD
An Art Deco-themed Italian with
an excellent selection of seafood,
meat dishes and wine.

PRICE CATEGORIES
For a three-course meal for one with half
a bottle of wine (or equivalent meal),
taxes and extra charges.
....
D Under AED 100 **DD** AED 100–400
DDD Over AED 400

---

6 Eauzone
MAP B2 ■ One&Only Royal
Mirage, Al Sufouh ■ 04 399 9999
■ Open noon–3:30pm & 7–11:30pm
■ DDD
Enjoy classic Pan-Asian dishes and
contemporary fine-dining creations
here *(see p46)* under tented canopies.

7 Trèsind
MAP B2 ■ One&Only Royal
Mirage, Al Sufouh ■ 056 420 9754
■ Open 12:30–3:30pm & 6:30–11pm
daily ■ DDD
Sample sophisticated Indian cuisine
in a charming setting. Trésind's menu
is created by Himanshu Saini, one of
Dubai's most acclaimed chefs.

8 Indego by Vineet
MAP B2 ■ Grosvenor House,
Dubai Marina ■ 04 317 6000 ■ Open
7–11:30pm daily ■ DDD
A contemporary take *(see p47)* on
traditional Indian cuisine overseen
by chef Vineet Bhatia, the first Indian
chef to be awarded a Michelin star.

9 City Social
MAP B2 ■ Grosvenor House,
Al Emreef St, Dubai Marina ■ 04 402
2222 ■ Open 6pm–2am Sun–Thu
(to 3am Fri & Sat) ■ DD
Celebrity chef Jason Atherton's
latest Dubai restaurant serves
elevated British comfort food.

10 Rhodes Twenty10
MAP B2 ■ Le Royal Méridien
Beach Resort ■ 04 316 5550 ■ Open
7pm–midnight ■ DDD
Formerly overseen by late UK chef
Gary Rhodes, this stylish restaurant
features a mix of British classics and
Middle Eastern-influenced dishes.

See map on p82 ←

TOP 10 Downtown Abu Dhabi

A stunning city of shiny new skyscrapers strung out along an idyllic corniche, oil-rich Abu Dhabi is the capital of the UAE and a rising player in the world's financial, commercial and tourist stages. Many visitors enjoy the slower and more traditional pace of life compared to Dubai, although after spending years in the shadow of its neighbour, Abu Dhabi has launched its own spectacular spate of large-scale developments, ranging from the ultra-opulent mock-Arabian Emirates Palace, one of the world's most lavish hotels, to the futuristic architecture of Al Maryah Island and the gleaming Etihad Towers. Downtown Abu Dhabi is the city's bustling commercial centre, where you'll find the biggest mega-developments, the liveliest attractions, and all the busiest shops, bars and restaurants.

The expansive Abu Dhabi Corniche

1 Abu Dhabi Corniche
MAP N1–R1

Abu Dhabi's showpiece boulevard sweeps for almost 5 km (3 miles) along the Downtown waterfront. A long line of skyscrapers rises to one side, while to the other are a series of gardens, popular in the evenings with strolling locals and joggers. Hiring a bike and riding up and down the waterfront is a great way to spend an hour or so, and there's a fine stretch of public beach.

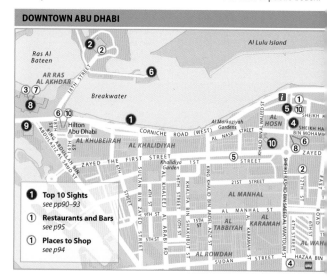

DOWNTOWN ABU DHABI

- **1** Top 10 Sights
  see pp90–93
- **1** Restaurants and Bars
  see p95
- **1** Places to Shop
  see p94

Looking across the water to Al Maryah Island and its new developments

② Marina Mall
MAP P1 ■ The Breakwater
■ **800 6623** ■ **Open 10am–10pm daily (until midnight Thu & Fri)**
■ **www.marinamall.ae**

Despite its slightly out-of-the way location, the sprawling Marina Mall is one of the city's largest and most popular shopping destinations, with shops laid out between an attractive sequence of circular atriums topped with tent-shaped roofs. The highlight of the complex is the slender Marina Sky Tower, at the back of the mall, which offers superb views over the city and Corniche from the Colombiano coffee shop (floor 41) or the Tiara revolving restaurant (floor 42).

③ Al Maryah Island
MAP T3

On the northern side of Downtown, this island is the site of arguably the city's most ambitious mega-project. Abu Dhabi's new financial and business district, the island is home to Abu Dhabi Global Market Square, a Four Seasons and a Rosewood hotel, the city's largest IMAX cinema and the chic Galleria mall (see p94).

④ World Trade Center
MAP R2 ■ Hamdan Bin
Mohammed St ■ **www.wtcad.ae**

One of the largest developments in Abu Dhabi, the World Trade Center is topped by the Trust Tower and the Burj Mohammed bin Rashid. The main attraction is its souk (see p94), offering a kind of postmodern re-imagining of the traditional Arabian souk.

The soaring World Trade Center

5 Al Ittihad Square
MAP R1

A crop of supersized sculptures stand in the small park at the centre of Al Ittihad Square, creating a whimsical contrast to the surrounding tower blocks. The five sculptures feature a gigantic coffeepot, a huge perfume bottle, an elaborate plate cover, a colossal cannon and a small fort.

Potter at Abu Dhabi Heritage Village

6 Abu Dhabi Heritage Village
MAP P1 ■ The Breakwater ■ 02 681 4455 ■ Open 9am–4pm Sat–Thu, 3:30–9pm Fri ■ www.visitabudhabi.ae

For a taste of life as it was in the city before the discovery of oil, Abu Dhabi's Heritage Village is the place to come. In a superb location directly over the water from the soaring towers of the Corniche, the village comprises a line of traditional *barasti* (palm-frond) huts, some of them turned into workshops in which resident craftspeople can sometimes be seen at work.

THE DISCOVERY OF OIL

The Japanese invention of the cultured pearl and the subsequent collapse of the Gulf's pearl industry led to the granting of petroleum concessions by Sheikh Shakhbut bin Sultan Al Nahyan in 1939. It turned out to be a very wise move. The discovery of oil in 1958 and its export from 1962 made Abu Dhabi an extremely rich city.

7 Al Mina Souks
MAP T1 ■ Al Mina ■ Open 5am–11pm daily

Stretching away on the northern side of Downtown Abu Dhabi is the city's Al Mina port area. A trio of small markets can be found here. The so-called Carpet Souk *(see p94)* comprises a small square with low-key shops. The nearby food souk is the heart of the city's retail trade in vegetables and fruit, while opposite is the lively fish market, with the day's catch laid out along the quay.

8 Emirates Palace
Abu Dhabi's magnificent pink palace hotel *(see pp30–31)* dominates the western end of the splendid Corniche. The majestic multi-domed exterior is surpassed in extravagance only by the dazzling interior which glitters with gold and sparkles with Swarovski crystals. The Emirates Palace was constructed to provide opulent accommodation fitting for the capital's visiting dignitaries.

Iconic façade of the Emirates Palace

9 Etihad Towers

MAP N2 ■ Observation deck at 300: Open 10am–6pm daily ■ Adm ■ www.etihadtowers.com

Dominating the southwestern end of the Corniche is the huge Etihad Towers development, a cluster of five glistening skyscrapers with gently curved outlines and a gleaming metallic shine. There are superlative views over Abu Dhabi from the 74th-floor Observation Deck at 300 (in tower two) and from Ray's Bar on the 62nd floor of the Jumeirah at Etihad Towers hotel (see p115).

Etihad Towers dominating the skyline

10 Qasr al Hosn

MAP R2 ■ Al Nasr St (5th St)

Located at the heart of Downtown, Qasr al Hosn (the Palace Fort) offers an unexpected throwback to earlier times. This is the oldest building in Abu Dhabi, first established back in the 1760s, after which it served as home to the ruling Al Nahyan family for the next two centuries. Most of what you see now – a high white wall dotted with a sequence of circular battlemented towers – was built in the 1940s. A highlight is the House of Artisans, where local crafts are explored through interactive workshops that teach traditions from basket weaving to embroidery.

A CORNICHE AND CITY WALK

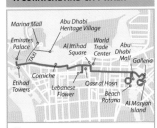

▶ MORNING

Start with a stroll around the stunning new Abu Dhabi Global Market Square (Sowwah Square) on **Al Maryah Island** (see p91) and a wander through the boutique shops of the **Galleria** (see p94). Afterwards, head along the waterfront before crossing the bridge to the Downtown area. Wander past the **Abu Dhabi Mall** (see p94) and along 5th St, one of the city's liveliest shopping areas, then have a look into the souk at the **World Trade Center** (see p91) and admire the quirky statues in **Al Ittihad Square**. From here it's a short stroll past **Qasr al Hosn** to the **Lebanese Flower** restaurant (see p95), where you can break for lunch.

AFTERNOON

Walk down past Al Markaziyah Gardens to the spectacular **Corniche** (see p90) and then take a stroll along a bit of the waterfront before jumping in a cab and heading past the **Etihad Towers** for afternoon tea in the opulent surroundings of the **Emirates Palace** hotel. Catch another cab for the short drive to the **Abu Dhabi Heritage Village**, after which you can watch the sun set from the top of the Sky Tower in the **Marina Mall** (see p91).

Catch a taxi back to Downtown and enjoy the spectacular night-time view of Al Maryah Island from the terrace of the fashionable Finz restaurant at the **Beach Rotana** hotel (see p116). End the day with a drink at the hotel's German-themed Brauhaus pub.

See map on pp90–91 ←

Places to Shop

① Abu Dhabi Mall
MAP T2 ▪ Tourist Club area
▪ 02 645 4858 ▪ Open 10am–10pm daily (until 11pm Thu & Fri) ▪ www.abudhabi-mall.com

Known as "AD Mall", this popular spot has all the top-name shops.

A water feature at Marina Mall

② Marina Mall
This enormous mall *(see p91)* is packed with stores, cinemas and cafés. There is even an ice rink.

③ Carpet Souk
MAP U2 ▪ Mina (Port) Rd

This souk is more about the buying experience than the items on offer (carpets, rugs, kilims and cushions).

④ Al Wahda Mall
MAP R3 ▪ Near Central Bus Stop ▪ 02 443 7070 ▪ Open 10am–10pm daily (until 11pm Thu–Sat) ▪ www.alwahda-mall.com

With more than 250 stores and a cinema hall, this recently expanded mall is now the largest in Abu Dhabi.

⑤ Iranian Souq
MAP U2 ▪ Mina (Port) Rd

Amid the plastic items and plants sold here, you'll find Iranian painted crafts.

⑥ Fotouh Al Khair Mall
MAP R2 ▪ Airport Rd ▪ Open 10am–10pm daily ▪ 02 622 2241 ▪ www.fotouhalkhairmall.com

Expats love this bright mini mall. It is home to Marks & Spencer and a number of other popular UK brands.

⑦ Khalifa Centre
MAP T2 ▪ 10th St, opposite Abu Dhabi Mall, Tourist Club area ▪ Open 10am–1pm & 4–10pm Sat–Fri ▪ 02 667 9900

Bargain here for exquisite Persian rugs, sheeshas, tribal kilims and even silver prayer boxes.

⑧ Hamdan St
MAP R2 ▪ Sheikh Hamdan bin Mohammed St (Hamdan St)

This street sells almost everything. It has jewellery stores and Arabic and Bollywood music shops, as well as discount supermarkets.

⑨ The Galleria
MAP T2 ▪ Al Maryah Island ▪ Open 10am–10pm daily (until midnight Thu & Fri) ▪ 02 616 6999 ▪ www.thegalleria.ae

Spanning three floors, the Galleria houses numerous luxury boutique stores from across the world.

⑩ World Trade Center Souk
MAP R2 ▪ Off Al Ittihad Square ▪ 02 508 2400 ▪ Open 10am–10pm daily (until 11pm Thu & Fri) ▪ www.wtcad.ae

Explore craft and souvenir shops at this stunning souk within the World Trade Center *(see p91)*. You can also buy local food, spices and honey here.

The World Trade Center Souk

Restaurants and Bars

PRICE CATEGORIES
For a three-course meal for one with half a bottle of wine (or equivalent meal), taxes and extra charges.

D Under AED 100 **DD** AED 100–400
DDD Over AED 400

1 Pickl
MAP R2 ■ World Trade Centre ■ 02 886 7314 ■ Open 11am–2am Sun–Thu (to 3am Fri & Sat) ■ D
Homegrown burger joint Pickl is famous for its juicy burgers, topped with a special secret sauce. Vegan options are also available.

2 Beijing
MAP N2 ■ Madinat Zayed ■ 02 621 0708 ■ Open 11am–midnight daily ■ D
Chinese food need not be expensive, as this popular spot pulls out all the stops to prove.

3 Hakkasan
MAP N6 ■ Emirates Palace Hotel, Corniche West St ■ 02 690 7999 ■ Open 6pm–midnight daily & noon–3pm Fri & Sat ■ DDD
This award-winning Chinese restaurant serves exquisite Cantonese staples. Its interiors have been designed by French interior designers Gilles & Boissier.

4 Zuma
Al Maryah Island ■ 02 401 5900 ■ Opening hours vary; call ahead ■ DD
A restaurant serving superb Japanese fare. Choose from a wide selection of dishes offered by the main kitchen, the robata grill, and the sushi counter.

5 Lebanese Flower
MAP P3 ■ Near Choitrams Supermarket, cnr Hamdan & Fourth St, Khalidya ■ 02 665 8700 ■ Open 8am–2am daily ■ No alcohol ■ D
A must-visit restaurant serving scrumptious mezze (Arabic appetizers), smoky mixed grilled meat plates and honey-soaked baklava.

6 Vasco's
MAP N2 ■ Hilton Abu Dhabi, Corniche Rd West ■ 02 681 1900 ■ Open noon–3.30pm & 7pm–11pm daily ■ DDD
A smart restaurant offering an incredible blend of European cooking with Asian influences.

Sayad, with views to the sea

7 Sayad
MAP N1 ■ Emirates Palace Hotel, Corniche Rd West ■ 02 690 7999 ■ Open 6:30–11:30pm daily ■ DDD
Expect playful decor and fine seafood cuisine at this swanky restaurant.

8 Royal Orchid
MAP T2 ■ The Galleria, Al Maryah Island ■ 02 677 9911 ■ Open noon–11:30pm daily ■ No alcohol ■ D
An authentic little Thai restaurant with a great atmosphere.

9 India Palace
MAP T2 ■ Al Salam St ■ 02 644 8777 ■ Open noon–midnight daily ■ No alcohol ■ D
Dine on North Indian cuisine in an opulent Anglo-Indian-style setting.

10 Jazz Bar & Dining
MAP P6 ■ Hilton Abu Dhabi, Corniche Rd West ■ 02 681 1900 ■ Open 7pm–2am daily (until 3am Thu & Fri)
Enjoy live jazz and great cocktails at this Art Deco-inspired bar.

See map on pp90–91

🔟 Beyond the Centre of Abu Dhabi

Car at Ferrari World

Beyond the central Downtown area, Abu Dhabi is booming. Beautiful beach-lined Saadiyat Island, a couple of miles east from the centre, is home to Louvre Abu Dhabi (a sister museum to the Louvre in Paris) and contemporary art gallery Manarat Al Saadiyat. The Guggenheim Abu Dhabi, Zayed National Museum and Natural History Museum will soon be new additions, cementing the destination's status as a cultural hub. Past here, adjacent Yas Island is where you will find the city's famous Formula 1 racetrack and swanky Yas Marina, with the vast Ferrari World and Yas Waterworld theme parks close by. Back towards the centre, the city shows its more traditional face at the vast white Sheikh Zayed Mosque, one of the world's most spectacular modern mosques.

BEYOND THE CENTRE OF ABU DHABI

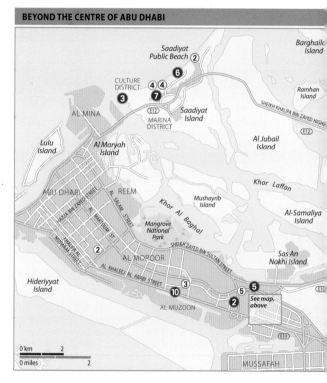

1 Bain al Jessrain
MAP V4 ■ Souk Qaryat al Beri: Open 10am–10pm Sat–Thu, 4–10pm Fri ■ www.soukqaryatalberi.com

Most of Abu Dhabi is actually built on an island separated from the mainland by a narrow sea inlet known as Maqta Creek – it wasn't until the opening of Maqta Bridge in 1966 that the island and mainland were connected. Three bridges span the creek, whose shores feature several top hotels and some of the city's most valuable real estate. The area on the mainland side, known as Bain al Jessrain (Between the Bridges), is also where you'll find the little Souk Qaryat al Beri, which houses a string of multiple boutique and eating outlets set over two levels. Following a Venetian theme, canals meander throughout the pretty souk.

The striking Sheikh Zayed Mosque

2 Sheikh Zayed Mosque
This impressive structure (see pp28–9) is an imposing sight along the drive from Dubai to Abu Dhabi. The mosque is named after Sheikh Zayed bin Sultan Al Nahyan, the founder and the first president of the United Arab Emirates, who is also buried here. The building is open to non-Muslims, but visitors should dress appropriately.

3 Louvre Abu Dhabi
MAP V2 ■ Cultural District, Abu Dhabi ■ Adm ■ www.louvre-abudhabi.ae

A branch of the famous Parisian museum, and one of the largest art museums in the Arabian peninsula, this is the centrepiece of the Saadiyat Cultural District today. The building was designed by French architect Jean Nouvel and resembles a seemingly weightless, enormous silvery flying saucer under an intricately latticed roof that allows light to enter into the museum through perforations. The museum hosts a range of rotating exhibits from the Louvre's collections, including a strong selection of Middle Eastern and Islamic art, and also organizes film screenings frequently.

Pure white sand and turquoise-blue sea at Saadiyat Public Beach

4 Yas Waterworld
MAP W4 ▪ Yas Island
▪ 02 414 2000 ▪ Open 10am–7pm daily ▪ Adm; under 3s free ▪ www.yaswaterworld.com

Rivalling Wild Wadi (see p78) and Aquaventure (see p84) in Dubai, Abu Dhabi's state-of-the-art water park offers more than 40 stomach-churning rides and slides, plus gentler water-based fun for kids and adults alike. Adrenaline junkies should head for the near-vertical Jebel Drop water slide. The nearby Yas Public Beach has loads of sand, an infinity pool and lovely loungers to relax on.

A jumble of slides, Yas Waterworld

5 Al Maqtaa Fort
MAP V4 ▪ Al Maqtaa bridge, on the right coming from Dubai

This small 200-year-old fort once guarded the main approach to the city and still stands sentinel beside Al Maqtaa Bridge. The sand-coloured exterior is adorned with carved wooden doors and shuttered windows, with narrow slits above for rifles.

6 Saadiyat Public Beach
MAP V2 ▪ Open 8am–sunset daily ▪ Adm with lounger and umbrella

This beautiful beach offers a nice change of pace from the city centre, with a huge expanse of fine white sand. The dunes behind the beach are a nesting site for turtles and a refuge for other rare flora and fauna, while dolphins are sometimes spotted offshore here. The facilities include toilets, showers and a café.

7 Manarat al Saadiyat
MAP V2 ▪ Sheikh Khalifa Hwy
▪ Open 9am–8pm daily ▪ 02 657 5800
▪ manaratalsaadiyat.ae

Great things are planned for Saadiyat Island, although it's likely to be quite a few years before the development really gets going. In the meantime, a sense of the enormous ambitions of this project-in-progress can be gleaned from a visit to Manarat al Saadiyat, hosting tantalising architectural models and other exhibits on the future island. The striking metallic building next door is the UAE Pavilion, designed by Foster + Partners for the Shanghai World Expo in 2010.

8 Ferrari World
MAP W4 ▪ Yas Island
▪ 600 511115 ▪ Open 11am–8pm daily (until 10pm Thu–Sat) ▪ Adm; under 3s free ▪ www.ferrariworldabudhabi.com

The ultimate shrine to one of the world's most famous cars – appropriate enough in a city built almost entirely using petrodollars. Billing itself as the "world's largest indoor theme park" this vast red extravaganza has an amazing range of rides. Highlights include a Formula 1 simulator, the world's fastest rollercoaster and the vertiginous Tower of Speed ride.

9 Aldar HQ
MAP W4 ■ Al Raha, next to the Dubai–Abu Dhabi highway

The Aldar HQ is another strong contender for the title of Abu Dhabi's most unusual building. It is clearly visible from the main highway as you approach from Dubai. Claimed to be the world's first circular sky-scraper, the structure looks a lot like a huge magnifying glass, supported by a diagonal grid of steel girders. Casual visitors are welcome to go inside for a look at the airy atrium.

10 Capital Gate
MAP U3 ■ Al Khaleej al Arabi St

The so-called "Leaning Tower of Abu Dhabi", Capital Gate is one of the most remarkable of Abu Dhabi's many strange modern buildings. Officially recognized by Guinness World Records as the world's most tilted tower, this enormous skyscraper looks as if it's on the point of toppling headfirst into the sea, with four times more lean than even the famously wonky Leaning Tower of Pisa.

The tilting Capital Gate

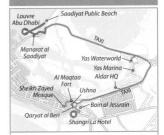

A DAY AROUND ABU DHABI

Louvre Abu Dhabi · *Saadiyat Public Beach* · *TAXI* · *Manarat al Saadiyat* · *Yas Waterworld* · *Yas Marina* · *Aldar HQ* · *Al Maqtaa Fort* · *Sheikh Zayed Mosque* · *Ushna* · *Bain al Jessrain* · *TAXI* · *Qaryat al Beri* · *Shangri La Hotel*

▶ MORNING

Spend the morning exploring the myriad treasures of the **Louvre Abu Dhabi** *(see p97)*, including a large selection of Middle Eastern and Islamic art. Afterwards, pop into the nearby **Manarat al Saadiyat** exhibition to see what the future of Abu Dhabi looks like. If museums aren't your thing, spend some time on the sands at **Saadiyat Public Beach** or brave the looping rides and slides of **Yas Waterworld**. Pick up some lunch either in the museum or at one of the numerous places to eat around the **Yas Marina**.

AFTERNOON

Next, head back to the mainland. If you have time, make a short detour to see the innovative **Aldar HQ** building en route. Spend the rest of the afternoon visiting the iconic **Sheikh Zayed Mosque** and admiring its incredibly ornate courtyard and interior.

As evening approaches, catch a cab for the short drive over to **Bain al Jessrain**. Look out for the 200-year-old **Al Maqtaa Fort** and then dive into **Qaryat al Beri** souk to explore the boutiques and restaurants there. Watch the sun go down over the historic Maqtaa Creek whilst sipping a cocktail at the kitsch **Ushna** *(see p101)*. Afterwards, head to one of the many excellent restaurants in the area. Bord Eau *(see p101)* at the **Shangri La Hotel** is an especially memorable place for a romantic evening meal, boasting sweeping views across the creek from the terrace.

See map on pp96–7 ←

Bars

Y Bar, with its striking brick-vaulted ceiling and modern seating area

1 Y Bar
MAP W4 ▪ Yas Island Rotana Hotel ▪ 02 656 4000 ▪ Open noon–2am daily ▪ www.rotana.com

A funky bar with an outdoor terrace. It's a great place for evening cocktails.

2 Cabana 9, Saadiyat Beach Club
MAP V2 ▪ Saadiyat Island ▪ 02 656 3500 ▪ Open 10am–sunset daily ▪ www.saadiyatbeachclub.ae

Sip a drink overlooking the sea at this idyllic beachfront pool bar.

3 Relax@12
MAP V3 ▪ Aloft Hotel, Khaleej al Arabi St ▪ 02 654 5138 ▪ Open 5pm till late daily ▪ www.relaxat12abudhabi.com

A cool rooftop bar with sweeping views. Visiting DJs keep things lively.

4 Buddha-Bar Beach Abu Dhabi
MAP V2 ▪ The St. Regis Saadiyat Island Resort ▪ 02 498 8888 ▪ Opening times vary, call ahead

A legendary pub providing a beach-themed experience in Abu Dhabi with tropical interiors and creative cocktails.

5 Poolside
MAP V4 ▪ Fairmont Bab Al Bahr, Khor Al Maqta ▪ 02 654 3333 ▪ Open 9am–6pm daily

This pool bar is the best place to soak up creek views and sip tasty cocktails, alongside gourmet burgers.

6 Stars 'N' Bars
MAP W4 ▪ Yas Island, Abu Dhabi ▪ 02 565 0101 ▪ Open 11:30am–2am daily

Enjoy varied international cuisine along with free arcade games at this American-style sports bar.

7 Sorso
MAP V4 ▪ Ritz Carlton ▪ 02 818 8888 ▪ Open 5pm–1am daily ▪ www.ritzcarlton.com

A smart bar that looks like the lounge of an old-school European gentlemen's club, with huge armchairs and plush sofas.

8 Belgian Beer Café
MAP W4 ▪ Radisson Blu Hotel, Yas Island ▪ 02 656 2000 ▪ Open noon–2am Sat–Wed, noon–3am Thu & Fri

A chic café serving lunch and dinner favourites accompanied by a fine selection of Belgian beverages.

9 Iris
MAP W4 ▪ Yas Yacht Club, Yas Marina ▪ 055 160 5636 ▪ Open 6pm–3am Mon–Sat ▪ www.yasmarina.ae

Pose with a drink at this chic bar-club, while admiring views of Yas Marina.

10 Wet Deck
MAP W4 ▪ W Abu Dhabi – Yas Island ▪ 02 656 0000 ▪ Open 6pm–1am daily (May–Sep: 8pm–2am daily) ▪ www.marriott.com

A hip venue set under a dramatic latticed roof, with a nightly DJ.

See map on pp96–7

Restaurants

1 Bord Eau
MAP V4 ▪ Shangri-La Hotel, Qaryat Al Beri ▪ 02 509 8555 ▪ Open 6:30–11:30pm daily ▪ DDD

This elegant French restaurant in the Shangri-La Hotel offers classic French dishes and modern, innovative cuisine. There is also a really excellent wine list.

2 Sardinia
MAP U3 ▪ Abu Dhabi Country Club ▪ 02 657 7640 ▪ Open noon–3pm & 7–11pm daily ▪ DD

An award-winning kitchen serving top-notch international cuisine. A complimentary amuse-bouche is served between each course.

3 Entrecôte Café de Paris
MAP V4 ▪ Shangri-La Hotel, Souk Qaryat al Beri ▪ 02 557 6508 ▪ Open noon–midnight daily ▪ DD

An offshoot of the famous Geneva restaurant, serving just a single dish – the famed entrecôte fillet steak – in the café's special secret sauce.

4 Amici
MAP W4 ▪ W Abu Dhabi – Yas Island ▪ 02 656 0000 ▪ Open 12:30–3pm & 7–11pm daily ▪ DD

An Italian restaurant serving freshly made pasta and wood-fired pizza, plus good antipasti.

5 Atayeb
MAP W4 ▪ W Abu Dhabi – Yas Island ▪ 02 656 0000 ▪ Open 7pm–1am Sun–Fri ▪ DD

This intimate restaurant (with a spectacular outdoor terrace) offers a rich array of classic Levantine dishes from Lebanon and Syria, cooked over charcoal stoves.

6 Hoi An
MAP V4 ▪ Shangri-La Hotel, Qaryat Al Beri ▪ 02 509 8555 ▪ Open 6–11:30pm daily ▪ DD

A smart colonial-style restaurant dishing up great Vietnamese cuisine.

PRICE CATEGORIES

For a three-course meal for one with half a bottle of wine (or equivalent meal), taxes and extra charges.

D Under AED 100 **DD** AED 100–400 **DDD** Over AED 400

---

7 Shang Palace
MAP V4 ▪ Shangri-La Hotel, Qaryat Al Beri ▪ 02 509 8555 ▪ Open noon–3pm & 7–11:30pm daily ▪ DD

Enjoy excellent Chinese cuisine cooked with panache.

8 Cipriani
MAP W4 ▪ Yas Yacht Club, Yas Marina ▪ 02 657 5400 ▪ Open 6pm–midnight daily ▪ DD

Enjoy an à la carte menu of Venetian and Italian cuisine prepared with seasonal ingredients.

9 Ushna
MAP V4 ▪ Souk Qaryat al Beri ▪ 02 559 9747 ▪ Open 12:30–11pm daily ▪ DD

A chic North Indian restaurant in an attractive waterside setting.

10 Angar
MAP W4 ▪ W Abu Dhabi – Yas Island ▪ 02 656 0000 ▪ Open 7pm–11am Wed–Mon, 2pm–11am Fri ▪ DD

A stylish and upmarket restaurant serving innovative and delicately spiced modern Indian cuisine.

Interior of the sophisticated Angar

Streetsmart

Al Fahidi Metro Station, Bur Dubai

Getting Around

Arriving by Air

Centrally located just outside the old city, sleek **Dubai Airport** is one of the world's best. **Emirates Airline** has its own, ultramodern terminal (3), while most other long-haul international flights land at Terminal 1.

Abu Dhabi Airport is also very modern in design and international visitors will arrive into an unusual circular terminal (1).

If you're from one of the countries eligible for an on-the-spot visa (see p106), the entry process is a breeze. If you don't come from an eligible country, make sure you have your visa documents to hand. Be aware that the UAE has very strict narcotics laws, and some prescription drugs are banned. Check customs information before flying, as you may have to ask your doctor for documentation.

There are almost always plenty of taxis at both airports. In Dubai the fixed rate from the airport is AED 25, with a fare into Deira or Bur Dubai of around AED 60, or into Jumeirah for AED 85–100. Alternatively, Terminals 1 and 3 are both connected to the Dubai Metro. There are also various airport buses including the useful **Sky Bus (Terhab)** network, which runs 24 hours from all three airport terminals with departures every 30 minutes. This is useful if you arrive at night when the metro isn't running. To get from Abu Dhabi air-

port, you'll either have to catch a taxi (around AED 70–80 into the city centre) or ride the 24-hour airport bus #A1, which runs regularly into the centre (AED 4). It's around a 30–40 minute drive into the city, depending on traffic.

Arriving by Road

The UAE's land borders with Saudi Arabia are open only to Gulf Corporation Council (GCC) nationals. There are five border crossings with Oman currently open, with visas issued on the spot to citizens of 49 countries (see p106).

Arriving by Sea

Numerous cruise ships include Dubai in their itineraries, docking at the **Dubai Cruise Terminal** in Port Rashid, centrally located between Jumeirah and Bur Dubai.

Travelling by Metro

All public land transport in Dubai is controlled by **RTA**. The impressive driverless Dubai Metro is by far the quickest and cheapest way to get around. There are two lines, Red and Green, which between them cover most of the city's sights. Trains run daily from around 5:30am to midnight (later on Thursday) and from 10am on Friday. There are departures every five to ten minutes. Children under five or shorter than 0.9m travel free. All trains have a plusher and more expensive Gold Class

compartment and a dedicated carriage for women and children.

Travelling by Tram

The superb **Dubai Tram** loops around the marina and continues up the coast for several kilometres, providing access to places the metro doesn't reach. The system connects directly to the metro and also links to the Palm Monorail (see p85).

Travelling by Bus

Dubai Buses, run by RTA, has an extensive bus network, although services tend to cover routes and areas of little interest to most visitors. Abu Dhabi buses (**DoT**) are more useful, with various routes criss-crossing Downtown. Fares are around AED 3–4 per journey. There are also regular bus services between the two cities, and to other major destinations across the country.

Transport Tickets

Run by RTA, almost all public transport in Dubai, including the metro, tram and city buses, is covered by the **Nol** ticketing system. Buy tickets before travelling; none are sold on board any form of transport. The cheapest option is the reusable Nol Red Ticket (AED 2). To use this you need to pre-pay the correct fare for each journey you make. You can also use it to buy a one-day travel pass (AED 20), offering unlimited transport around the city. There are also three types of rechargeable Nol cards (Silver, Gold and Blue) which can be pre-loaded with up to AED 500 of credit. Cards/tickets can be bought and topped up at any metro station and various other locations.

Travelling by Car

Driving in Dubai can be challenging, given the sometimes heavy traffic, labyrinthine road layouts and often aggressive driving styles, but is feasible if you're confident behind the wheel. Cars drive on the right, and speed limits are 60km/h (37 mph) on city streets, 80km/h (50 mph) on major city roads, and 100–120km/h (62–74 mph) on highways. Drinking and driving is a punishable offence and receives severe penalties. There are car-rental desks at airports, hotels and other locations. The international car-rental companies **Avis** and **Europcar** are well represented.

Travelling by Taxi

Taxis in both Dubai and Abu Dhabi can be hailed anywhere on the street, and there are taxi ranks at most shopping malls – although during busy times it might be better to call ahead. All taxis use meters and cost around AED 1.5 per km plus flag fall. In Dubai the flag fall is AED 5, with a minimum charge of AED 12 per ride. In Abu Dhabi the flag fare is AED 3.50 (AED 4 at night; minimum fare AED 10dh from 10pm to 6am). Reputable companies are the **Dubai Taxi Corporation** and **TransAD** (for Abu Dhabi). **Uber** also operates in both cities.

Travelling by Boat

The plush **Dubai Ferry** runs three times daily between Bur Dubai and Dubai Marina (75 minutes), and there are also various sightseeing round trips. Fares on all trips are AED 50. In the old city, *abras* criss-cross Dubai Creek, connecting Deira and Bur Dubai. The fare is AED 1 per person.

Cycling

In both Dubai and Abu Dhabi, bikes can be hired through **Byky**. Cycling infrastructure is improving in Dubai, with camel tracks at Nad Al Sheba converted into cycle lanes offering fantastic views of the city, and the Al Qudra Cycle Track stretching out into the surrounding desert.

Walking

Neither Dubai nor Abu Dhabi is very pedestrian friendly, though more pedestrianized areas and well maintained footpaths are appearing. Dubai's souks, marinas and Al Fahidi, and the Corniche, Al Raha Beach, and the Cultural District in Abu Dhabi are all excellent places to walk.

DIRECTORY

ARRIVING BY AIR

Abu Dhabi Airport
w abudhabiairport.ae

Dubai Airport
w dubaiairports.ae

Emirates Airline
w emirates.com

Sky Bus (Terhab)
w dubai-buses.com

ARRIVING BY SEA

Dubai Cruise Terminal
w dubaicruiseterminal.com

TRAVELLING BY METRO

RTA
w rta.ae

TRAVELLING BY TRAM

Dubai Tram
w alsufouhtram.com

TRAVELLING BY BUS

DoT
w dot.abudhabi.ae

TRANSPORT TICKETS

Nol
w rta.ae

TRAVELLING BY CAR

Avis
w avis.com

Europcar
w europcardubai.com
w europcar-abudhabi.com

TRAVELLING BY TAXI

Dubai Taxi Corporation
w dubaitaxi.ae

TransAD
w transad.ae

Uber
w uber.com

TRAVELLING BY BOAT

Dubai Ferry
w dubai-ferry.com

CYCLING

Byky
w q8byky.com

Practical Information

Passports and Visas

Free 30-day (90-day for some nationalities) visit visas are available on arrival for some countries, outlined on the **General Directorate of Residency and Foreigners Affairs** website. Passports must be valid for six months from the date of entry to the UAE. Visas for 30 days (but not for 90 days) can be extended by the General Directorate.

Canada, the UK, the US, and other countries have consular representation in the region. Check your consulate's UAE website for travel warnings and security information.

Government Advice

Now more than ever, it is important to consult both your and the UAE government's advice before travelling. The **UK Foreign, Commonwealth and Development Office**, the **US State Department**, the **Australian Department of Foreign Affairs and Trade** and the **UAE Government Portal** offers the latest information on security, health and local regulations.

Customs Information

You can find information on the laws relating to goods and currency taken in or out of the UAE on the **Dubai Customs** website. The duty-free allowance for each traveller is 400 cigarettes, 500g (18 oz) of tobacco, 50 cigars and 4 litres of alcohol. Alcohol cannot be bought from local shops without a liquor licence (only available to UAE residents), so buy duty free at the airport if you want to have your own supply at home.

In addition to the usual items (firearms, illegal drugs and pornography), it is forbidden to bring in any banned movies, TV programs and offensive publications, especially films and programs that may include scenes with passionate kissing, sex, nudity or semi-nudity, or drug use. Goods made in Israel (or bearing Israeli logos) are also forbidden.

Insurance

We recommend that you take out a comprehensive insurance policy covering theft, loss of belongings, medical care, cancellations and delays, and read the small print carefully. While petty crime is rare in the UAE, an insurance policy provides peace of mind.

Health

The UAE has a world-class healthcare system, with highly efficient hospitals, but services are expensive. Full health insurance, arranged before your trip, is advised.

No special vaccinations are required for the UAE, though a COVID-19 vaccine certificate is recommended. Tap water is safe to drink. At most, you may initially experience an upset stomach as your body adjusts to new bacteria. Standards are outstanding in both private and public hospitals, although the services are generally faster at the emergency departments at private hospitals. Good hospitals for tourists include the **American Hospital** and **Emirates Hospital** in Dubai, and the **Burjeel Hospital** and **Cleveland Clinic** in Abu Dhabi.

There are numerous pharmacies, including many that open 24 hours (ask at your hotel for the nearest branch).

Smoking, Alcohol and Drugs

Smoking is prohibited in bars, restaurants, clubs and cafés. It is also forbidden to smoke on public transport. Some of these places and means of transport may have designated smoking areas, but these should be closely obeyed. You will see many bars offering shisha, which is legal for users over the age of 18.

Generally, the legal drinking age in Abu Dhabi is 18, but a by-law prevents hotels from serving alcohol to those under the age of 21. In Dubai the drinking age is 21. It is prohibited to drive under the influence of alcohol or other substances; those caught doing so will be fined and may temporarily or permanently lose their driving licence.

Penalties for the use and trafficking of drugs are severe, with fines and sentences often imposed.

ID

You will need photo ID when buying alcohol, and often for entry into bars and night clubs. It is not a legal requirement to carry picture ID at all times but a valid driving licence will be required if you want to rent a car.

Personal Security

It is important to exercise caution when visiting the UAE. Although people of all races and religions are welcome, it is an Islamic state and you can land in trouble for not respecting local religious customs and decency laws.

Arrests have resulted from foreigners being too affectionate in public. If you get arrested, do not sign anything in Arabic immediately. Your consulate should be your first call – they can help facilitate contact with a local bilingual lawyer.

Homosexuality is illegal and punishable with harsh penalties, although very rarely enforced. Though both Dubai and Abu Dhabi have large expat communities who may be more accepting of all people, it is unfortunately still important to keep in mind state law and to act accordingly. You may see men from Central Asia and the Indian Sub-continent holding hands – this common act signifies friendship.

Women travelling solo in the UAE shouldn't experience any harassment if they follow local norms. Sit in the back seat of taxis and in the "women's section"

of buses. Dedicated women's queues at banks and government departments indicate that women will get preferential service.

While petty crime is almost unheard of, be sensible – don't leave valuables unattended. **Ambulance, police and fire services** can be easily contacted in emergencies.

As a pedestrian be vigilant; drivers will not stop for you on a crossing, so cross only at lights where possible. If your taxi driver is driving too fast or recklessly, tell them to slow down ("shway shway").

In Dubai, if you leave something behind in a taxi, you'll need to file a report at Dubai Taxi. For any other lost property, contact the Police Lost and Found.

If you're driving and you have an accident, first get out of harm's way, then call the police for instructions. Decelerate or pull over in sand storms when visibility is poor.

When swimming, take warning signs regarding dangerous rips and strong undertows seriously. In spite of the water's calm appearance, Dubai's beaches have very powerful undercurrents.

Casual irritations while visiting Dubai include the numerous touts in old city souks attempting to sell "copy watches" or "copy bags" and so on. These industries can be highly unethical. Male visitors might also be solicited by sex workers in bars, especially in the older parts of the city later in the evenings.

DIRECTORY

PASSPORTS AND VISAS

General Directorate of Residency and Foreigners Affairs
Ⓦ gdrfad.gov.ae

GOVERNMENT ADVICE

Australian Department of Foreign Affairs and Trade
Ⓦ smartraveller.gov.au

UAE Government Portal
Ⓦ u.ae/en

UK Foreign, Commonwealth and Development Office
Ⓦ gov.uk/foreign-travel-advice

US Department of State
Ⓦ travel.state.gov

CUSTOMS INFORMATION

Dubai Customs
Ⓦ dubaicustoms.gov.ae

HEALTH

American Hospital
Ⓒ 04 337 5500
Ⓦ ahdubai.com

Burjeel Hospital
Ⓒ 04 407 0100 (Dubai)
Ⓒ 02 508 5555 (Abu Dhabi)
Ⓦ burjeel.com

Cleveland Clinic
Ⓒ 04 313 9999, 800 5111, 800 82223
Ⓦ clevelandclinicabudhabi.ae

Emirates Hospital
Ⓒ 04 520 0500, 800 444 444
Ⓦ emirateshospital.ae

EMERGENCY SERVICES

Ambulance
Ⓒ 999

Fire
Ⓒ 997

Police
Ⓒ 999

Travellers with Specific Requirements

Developers have worked hard to cater to visitors with specific requirements in many of Dubai and Abu Dhabi's newest hotels and resorts. Infrastructure in the cities is generally wheelchair accessible, including most buses and trains. Most of the more modern and upmarket hotels now have specially adapted rooms, although this can be harder to find in cheaper accommodation.

There are excellent transport services at both airports for visitors with disabilities, while the Dubai Metro boasts tactile guide paths, wheelchair spaces in compartments and other facilities. The **Visit Dubai** website has pages dedicated to accessible travel, and can direct you to helpful resources when visiting the UAE.

Time Zone

The UAE time zone is GMT+4. It is 9 hours ahead of North American Eastern Standard Time, 12 hours ahead of North American Western Standard Time, and 6 hours behind Australian Eastern Standard Time. There is no daylight saving.

Money

The UAE's currency is the United Arab Emirates dirham, written as AED or Dh. One dirham is divided into 100 fils. Currency notes are in denominations of AED 5, AED 10, AED 20, AED 50, AED 100, AED 200, AED 500 and AED 1000. Coins are available as 25 fils, 50 fils and one dirham. The UAE dirham is pegged to the US dollar. US$1 is equal to AED 3.67. All other currencies fluctuate, but at the time of writing €1 was equal to AED 4 and £1 was worth AED 5.

Numerous international banks operate in the UAE, including HSBC, Citibank and Standard Chartered Bank. Good local banks include National Bank of Abu Dhabi, Mashreq Bank and Emirates National Bank of Dubai. Globally linked ATMs are located everywhere. American Express, Mastercard and Visa are widely accepted, and credit cards and contactless payments can be used almost anywhere.

There are also several bureaux de change, such as the leading **Al Ansari Exchange**, which has branches all over the city, including in many malls. Bringing cash from home and changing it locally is often cheaper than using plastic, which can mean having to pay hefty credit card and ATM fees.

Although tipping is not common or expected it is always appreciated.

Electrical Appliances

UAE power sockets generally accept the UK three-prong plug operating on 220/240 volts, although you may also see the European two-round-prong plug. It's a good idea to bring an adaptor that works for both to be safe. Some hotels have adaptors you can borrow, or you can buy them in supermarkets.

Mobile Phones and Wi-Fi

To phone the UAE from abroad, dial your international access code, the UAE country code 971, then 4 for Dubai or 2 for Abu Dhabi, followed by the local number. To dial a mobile from abroad, dial 971 50/55/56 followed by the mobile number. Within the UAE, dial 050/055/056 for mobiles, 04 to call Dubai from outside the emirate and 02 to phone Abu Dhabi from another emirate.

If you need a mobile, it's generally easier (and cheaper) to get a local SIM card. The national telecommunications company Etisalat offers visitors a useful "Visitor Mobile Line", which gives you a SIM card and allows you to make calls at local rates. The card is available at the Etisalat shops and other outlets. You will need to present your passport when purchasing a SIM card.

There is WiFi access everywhere. Etisalat operates numerous WiFi "hotspots" in shopping malls, restaurants, coffee shops and elswhere. You can pay online with a credit card, with rates starting at around AED 15 per hour.

Postal Services

Emirates Post is the UAE's national postal service. You can buy stamps at any post office and at some stationery shops. Mail to Europe, North America and Australasia takes about 10 days. It is unreliable, however, so register anything valuable or use a courier for anything urgent. Emirates Post also provides surface and air delivery services for sending large parcels, although courier services are more reliable. Postal companies with a good reputation for service include **Aramex** and **FedEx**. All will pick up from your hotel. You can pay on collection if you don't have an account.

Weather

The UAE has an arid desert climate with infrequent rainfall. Temperatures average 20°C (68°F) in the winter to 45°C (113°F) in the summer. Winter (December to January) is usually when Dubai is at its best and busiest, although you may experience a little rain and overcast skies. This is when the Dubai Shopping Festival, Global Village and most major sporting events take place. October to November and March to April are a bit hotter and are almost guaranteed sunshine. Summer (May to September) is scorching and it's almost impossible to do anything except lounge by a pool or stay in air-conditioned buildings, although hotel prices tumble dramatically.

Opening Hours

The UAE weekend is Friday and Saturday. Business hours aren't fixed but, generally, shopping malls and supermarkets are open daily 10am–10pm (sometimes later on weekends). Shops in the streets open at approximately the same times but often close for lunch from 1 to 4/5pm. Take advantage of the regular happy hours at restaurants (generally 6pm–8pm daily). Government departments open around 7am and close to the public around 3pm. Opening hours for museums fluctuate wildly, and some smaller places close during the afternoon.

The holy month of Ramadan presents some challenges to visitors. Although you are not expected to join the fasting, you should be tolerant of those who are practising their faith during these weeks.

Over the past three years, laws for food establishments during Ramadan have become more relaxed; bars and restaurants generally remain open as usual, particularly in the more popular tourist areas.

The COVID-19 pandemic proved that situations can change suddenly. Always check before visiting attractions and hospitality venues for up-to-date hours and booking requirements

Visitor Information

The **Department of Tourism and Commerce Marketing (DTCM)** oversees tourism in Dubai, while the **Abu Dhabi Tourism and Culture Authority (ADTCA)** is in charge in Abu Dhabi. For information on the latest events and happenings, *Time Out Dubai* and *Time Out Abu Dhabi* websites are great resources. **800Tickets** sell tickets for many major music (and other) events. *What's On* magazine is also handy. For Dubai, **The Entertainer** app is great for deals, discounts, services and information.

Sustainable Travel

The UAE has one of the largest ecological footprints in the world, but the government are working to enhance their sustainable practices. The Dubai Department of Tourism and Commerce Marketing have launched a "Green Tourism Award" program to encourage eco-tourism. This has led to many travel providers devoting more time and attention to lessening the carbon footprint of the services they offer.

When visiting, travellers are advised to seek out activities with lower emissions. Rather than taking cars through the desert, a whole host of activities are available, including hiking and camping in the Hajar Mountains, scuba and snorkeling outings on the UAE's coast, or bird-watching adventures.

Language

The official language of the United Arab Emirates is Arabic, with Modern Standard Arabic taught in schools. The majority of native Emiratis speak a Gulf Arabic dialect that is broadly similar to that spoken in other countries in the region.

A broad array of languages are spoken among the large and diverse expatriate community, including dialects of Pashto, Hindi, and Balochi. You will also hear Persian. English is the most widely spoken language in Dubai, and is also generally spoken and understood across Abu Dhabi.

Taxes and Refunds

The standard VAT rate in the UAE is 5 per cent on all taxable supplies and imports. Tourists and visitors are eligible for refunds on VAT paid on purchases they made during their stay.

Trips and Tours

There are dozens of tour operators in both Dubai and Abu Dhabi offering a varied range of desert outings, trips to neighbouring cities and dinner *dhow* cruises.

Arabian Adventures *(see p33)* is the biggest and best. The company has become increasingly committed to sustainability in recent years, with all of their desert safaris run by professionally trained guides with full knowledge of desert flora and fauna. Other tour providers offering safaris may not make the same guarantees, so ensure you check company sustainability and animal welfare credentials before placing a booking.

Hop-on hop-off sightseeing bus tours are run by **Big Bus Tours** in both Dubai and Abu Dhabi.

Abras, or water taxis, can be chartered *(see pp16–17)* for private cruises up and down the creek in Dubai. They also run frequently along two main routes, with two stations in Deira and two in Bur Dubai. Visit the **Dubai Online** website for timetables and more information. There are also sightseeing trips aboard the **Dubai Ferry**. Walking tours of Al Fahidi

are offered by the SMCCU *(see p19)*, and interesting foodie tours of offbeat Dubai eateries by **Frying Pan Adventures**. For a walk on the wild side in the mountains of the UAE and Oman, contact **Absolute Adventure** or **UAE Trekkers**.

Shopping

There are basically two types of shopping in Dubai and Abu Dhabi: modern malls and traditional souks. Shopping malls are found everywhere, from huge mega-developments to low-key local places. Many leading local and international shops have outlets in malls, and chains such as **Damas** (jewellery), **Paris Gallery** (perfume) and Grand Stores (electronics and cameras) can be found in almost all the major shopping centres. Prices are fixed and credit cards generally accepted.

Shopping in traditional souks in the old city is a different affair. Prices are generally lower and haggling is expected (credit cards may not be accepted except for big-ticket items). A lot of the items on sale consist of everyday essentials, but you'll also find interesting collectibles such as gold, spices, perfumes, designer fakes and antiques. Shops in Karama Souk *(see p27)* have a vast array of well-priced and convincing fakes, though be aware that these industries may not always be ethical.

Dining

There's a huge range of places to eat in both Dubai and Abu Dhabi, from inexpensive local cafés to extravagant fine-dining venues overseen by Michelin-starred chefs.

There's also a huge array of cuisines on offer. This is one of the best places to sample classic dishes from across the Middle East including traditional Arabian cuisine (or "Lebanese", as it is often described), along with Iranian, Moroccan and Emirati specialities. Indian, Italian and Chinese cuisine is also popular.

Cheaper places are aimed largely at Asian expats living in the city, hence the many Indian and Pakistani restaurants across the old city. Plenty of cafés serve Arabian food including *shawarma* kebabs in pitta bread.

More expensive places are largely attached to hotels and come in every possible shape and form, from opulent Arabian-themed venues to chic boltholes. Dining next to the sea is popular, and many places offer outdoor terraces – those with outdoor seating may also offer sheesha (waterpipes). Happy hours (typically from 6pm to 8pm) can make drinks much cheaper.

A 10 per cent service charge may be added to cover the tip, along with other taxes. These can add up to 25 per cent of the basic cost of a meal and drinks, so check before if included.

Children are generally well-catered for except at the very best fine-dining restaurants.

Accommodation

There's a mind-boggling array of accommodation in both Dubai and Abu Dhabi. The vast majority in both cities is generally found in large and almost exclusively modern hotels, although there are a few more characterful small hotels in historic houses in Dubai, including several places run by the Heritage Collection. You'll also find many Airbnb options and self-catering apartments. **Golden Sands** is the main local operator, with over a dozen apartment blocks in Bur Dubai.

There is considerable variety among the more upmarket hotels, with new resorts opening frequently. At the top end of the scale places range from chic modernist highrises through to lavish resorts built in opulent pseudo-Arabian style. Cheaper places, however, tend to be functional concrete boxes of rather uniform appearance. The main local chain is the luxurious, Dubai-owned **Jumeirah** group, although most of the world's leading hotel companies now have at least one establishment in each city, often several. Two of the most lavish resorts are run by **Atlantis**, with Atlantis, The Palm and the newer resort Atlantis, The Royal offering the highest standards of holiday accommodation.

Accommodation is available on all the usual booking websites. Check for hotel-plus-flight packages instead of both separately. Rates vary considerably from month to month (sometimes from week to week), peaking during the winter months and falling hugely during the summer *(see p109)*. During busy periods, such as the religious festival of Eid, hotel prices can soar. Rates start from around AED 275 (US$75) for a double in a old-city one-star hotel, rising up to tens of thousands of dollars per night at some of the world's most luxurious holiday resorts. Hotels quote room rates exclusive of relevant government taxes, which can bump the price up by 25 per cent. Be sure to always check the full price with tax before booking.

DIRECTORY

TRIPS AND TOURS

Absolute Adventure
04 392 6463
w adventure.ae

Big Bus Tours
w bigbustours.com

Dubai Ferry
w dubai-ferry.com

Dubai Online
w dubai-online.com/transport/abra

Frying Pan Adventures
w fryingpanadventures.com

UAE Trekkers
w uaetrekkers.com

SHOPPING

Damas
w damasjewellery.com

Paris Gallery
w parisgallery.com

ACCOMMODATION

Atlantis
w atlantis.com

Golden Sands
w goldensandsdubai.com

Jumeirah
w jumeirah.com

Places to Stay

PRICE CATEGORIES

For a standard, double room per night (with breakfast if included), taxes and extra charges.

D Under AED 600   DD AED 600–1500
DDD Over AED 1500

Luxury City Hotels in Dubai

Dusit Thani

MAP C6 ■ Sheikh Zayed Rd ■ 04 343 3333 ■ www. dusit.com ■ DD

What sets the Dusit apart is its gentle welcoming Thai hospitality, from the "Sawadee-ka" greeting to the Thai canapés. The spacious rooms cater well to the business traveller, but it's worth paying extra for Club Rooms.

Fairmont Dubai

MAP E5 ■ Sheikh Zayed Rd ■ 04 332 5555 ■ www. fairmont.com ■ DD

Convenient for business, shopping and sightseeing, the hotel's architecture and plush rooms ooze elegance and style.

Grosvenor House

MAP D6 ■ Dubai Marina ■ 04 399 8888 ■ www. grosvenorhouse-dubai. com ■ DD

Spacious well-appointed rooms at this swanky hotel have marina or sea views. Guests can use the beach and access water activities at its sister hotel, the Royal Meridien.

Jumeirah Emirates Towers

MAP C6 ■ Sheikh Zayed Rd ■ 04 330 0000 ■ www. jumeirahemiratestowers. com ■ DD

The city's most stylish business hotel occupies one of the two landmark Emirates Towers. The spectacular lobby is a sight in its own right, while the attached Boulevard mall has several good places to eat.

Radisson Blu Hotel, Dubai Deira Creek

MAP L2 ■ Baniyas Rd, Deira ■ 04 222 7171 ■ www.radissonblu. com ■ DD

The oldest five-star in the city, this hotel is centrally located, and has comfortable rooms and lovely creek views from small balconies. The superb selection of in-house restaurants and bars is one of the best in the city.

Shangri-La Dubai

MAP C5 ■ Sheikh Zayed Rd ■ 04 343 8888 ■ www. shangri-la.com ■ DD

One of Dubai's classiest city hotels, it offers immaculate service and has beautifully furnished rooms designed in contemporary Asian style, plus several excellent in-house restaurants.

Grand Hyatt Dubai

MAP E2 ■ Al Qataiyat Rd, Bur Dubai ■ 04 317 1234 ■ www.hyatt.com ■ DDD

With marvellous views over Creek Park across to the Dubai Creek Golf and Yacht Club, this massive property also has myriad attractions within the hotel. There's a wonderful interior rainforest garden with *dhow* bottoms embedded in the ceiling, and a variety of bars and restaurants.

Palace Downtown

MAP C6 ■ Downtown Burj Khalifa ■ 04 428 7888 ■ www.theaddress. com ■ DDD

Overlooking the Dubai Fountain, this luxurious offering is designed in lavish mock-Arabian style. Facilities include three international restaurants, a spa and excellent business facilities. Despite its close proximity to the busy Dubai Mall, a stay here still offers a calm and tranquil experience.

Luxury Beach Hotels in Dubai

Le Meridien Mina Seyahi Resort

MAP B2 ■ Al Sufouh Rd, Jumeirah ■ 04 399 3333 ■ www.marriott. com ■ DD

This dated resort hotel is nothing much to look at but has one of Dubai's best stretches of beachfront, backed by splendid palm-studded gardens dotted with several swimming pools. Rates are generally lower than in nearby places, making this one of the most affordable marina resorts.

Westin Mina Seyahi

MAP B2 ■ Al Sufouh Rd, Dubai Marina ■ 04 399 4141 ■ www.westinmina seyahi.com ■ DD

An elegant addition to Dubai's five-star coastline, Westin Mina Seyahi has spectacular views over the Arabian Gulf. The rooms are spacious and well-equipped; some, but not all, have balconies. Other facilities include a spa, gym, several bars and restaurants, and excellent water sports.

Atlantis, The Royal

MAP B1 ■ The Palm Jumeirah ■ www.atlantis. com/atlantis-the-royal ■ DDD
Designed to make Dubai's existing luxury resorts look like budget hostels, Atlantis, The Royal has every facility you would expect from a hotel of this calibre. All rooms have balconies, and some of the larger suites offer the absolute pinnacle of luxury accommodation.

Atlantis, The Palm

MAP B1 ■ The Palm Jumeirah ■ 04 426 0000 ■ www.atlantis thepalm.com ■ DDD
Located at the top of the Palm Jumeirah, this vast complex (see p84) has a wide choice of rooms, most with views over the Gulf. The ultimate in luxury, however, are the Lost Chambers suites with underwater views into the lagoon. Among the numerous facilities are a water park, a dolphinarium and a kids' club, making it ideal for families.

Burj Al Arab Jumeirah

MAP C1 ■ Jumeirah Rd ■ 04 301 7777 ■ www. jumeirah.com ■ DDD
Jutting into the sea, this iconic property provides the ultimate in personal attention – from your arrival in a Rolls Royce, to the staff greeting you in

the flamboyant foyer with welcome refreshments, cold towels, incense and dates, to the personal butler in your duplex suite. The interior is a little gaudy for some tastes, but the spectacular coastal views, especially from the Skyview Bar, make up for it.

FIVE Palm Jumeirah

MAP B1 ■ No. 1, Palm Jumeirah ■ 04 455 9999 ■ www.fivehotelsand resorts.com ■ DDD
Nestled in the iconic Palm Jumeirah, this resort offers a peek into the jet-setting lifestyle of Dubai's A-list crowd. Enjoy great drinks and stunning sunsets at The Penthouse, the roof-top pool club and lounge; and savour the flavours of Southern Italy at Quattro Passi, the Italian *ristorante*.

Jumeirah Al Qasr

MAP C2 ■ Madinat Jumeirah ■ 04 366 8888 ■ www.madinatjumeirah. com ■ DDD
The opulent Jumeirah Al Qasr resort ("the Jumeirah Palace" in Arabic) is graced with enormous wooden doors, elegant arches and charming Moroccan stone-work. Throughout the hotel you'll find *mashrabiya* screens, Moroccan lamps and lovely terracotta urns. There's also a gorgeous white-sand beach and views of the Mina A'Salam and Burj Al Arab Jumeirah.

Jumeirah Zabeel Saray

MAP B1 ■ Palm Jumeirah ■ 04 453 0000 ■ www. jumeirah.com ■ DDD
Despite its extravagant built and luxury service, this hotel often offers affordable rates. The outside looks like an

Ottoman palace, while the interior has many restaurants, bars and public areas, plus a private beach and an infinity pool.

Mina A'Salam

MAP C2 ■ Madinat Jumeirah ■ 04 366 8888 ■ www.madinatjumeirah. com ■ DDD
This resort's old-style Arabian architecture is inspired by the ancient towers of Yemen and Saudi Arabia, and by the wind-tower architecture of the Al Fahidi area in Dubai. Rooms have inlaid furni-ture, rich eastern lamps and Arabesque-patterned prints and tiles. Lattice balconies overlook the man-made waterways and splendid beach.

Nikki Beach Resort & Spa

MAP E1 ■ Pearl Jumeirah ■ 04 376 6162 ■ www. nikkibeach.com ■ DDD
An immaculate resort that stretches across the waterfront of Pearl Jumeirah. It is home to Café Nikki, a bistro famous for its Friday brunches, along with the popular Nikki Beach Club, known for a four-tier sheesha terrace and lounge.

One&Only Royal Mirage

MAP B2 ■ Al Sufouh Rd, Dubai Marina ■ 04 399 9999 ■ www.oneandonly resorts.com ■ DDD
One of the world's most romantic resorts, this exotic Moroccan-inspired hotel is set in palm-filled gardens with serene ponds. The white-sand beach has elegant white umbrellas and regal VIP canopies overlooking the Palm Jumeirah.

The Ritz-Carlton, Dubai

MAP B2 ▪ The Walk at JBR, Dubai Marina ▪ 04 399 4000 ▪ www.ritz carlton.com ▪ DDD

Dubai's sumptuous Ritz Carlton lives up to the reputation of the renowned chain, with lots of marble, chandeliers, Persian carpets and fresh flowers, and also palm-filled gardens and a white-sand beach.

Luxury Hotels in Abu Dhabi

Eastern Mangroves Hotel & Spa

MAP V3 ▪ Salam St ▪ 02 656 1000 ▪ www.abu-dhabi.anantara.com ▪ DD

This opulent waterfront resort, with its spectacular location, makes for a winning combination of luxury and nature. The Arabian-style interior is nicely done, and there's also a gorgeous spa and several fine restaurants.

Fairmont Bab al Bahr

MAP V4 ▪ Between the Bridges ▪ 02 654 3333 ▪ www.fairmont.com/babalbahr ▪ DD

Huge and homely five-star hotel, with sumptuous rooms and views over a creek and Sheikh Zayed Mosque. All rooms have lavish bathrooms, plus there's a fitness centre and a private beach. Chef Marco Pierre White has two restaurants here.

Intercontinental Abu Dhabi

MAP N2 ▪ Al Bateen St ▪ 02 666 6888 ▪ www.intercontinental.com ▪ DD

The Intercontinental is a spacious and relaxing

five-star option set at the quiet western end of Downtown. The idyllic beach and huge pool are a major draw, as are the in-house restaurants.

Jumeirah at Etihad Towers

MAP N2 ▪ Corniche Rd West ▪ 02 811 5555 ▪ www.jumeirah.com ▪ DD

One of Abu Dhabi's most chic addresses, occupying one of the five soaring Etihad Towers. Rooms here have a crisp contemporary design and all mod-cons.There's also a large private beach with three pools, and a spa.

Park Hyatt Abu Dhabi

MAP V2 ▪ Saadiyat Island ▪ 02 407 1234 ▪ www.hyatt.com ▪ DD

Located on a 9-km (6-mile) stretch of beach, with its own landscaped garden, the Park Hyatt has become one of Abu Dhabi's most desired locations. It is just a short drive from the city, but a world away in terms of tranquility. Camp Hyatt, housed within the hotel premises, is an exclusive facility offering fun activities for kids.

Shangri-La Qaryat Al Beri

MAP V4 ▪ Qaryat Al Beri ▪ 02 509 8888 ▪ www.shangri-la.com ▪ DD

Lavish Arabian-style hotel with rooms overlooking either the long private beach, or one of the swimming pools. It also has a lovely spa and fine restaurants, while all the amenities of the Souk Qaryat al Beri (see p97) are right next door.

Sofitel Abu Dhabi Corniche

MAP N1 ▪ Corniche Rd East ▪ 02 813 7777 ▪ sofitel.com ▪ DD

One of Downtown's newest and most alluring hotels, with plenty of cool contemporary style. The Art Déco-inspired high-rise building offers brilliant views from the upper floors, while the chic Jazz ´n Fizz Bar has become established as one of the area's most fashionable hangouts.

St Regis Saadiyat Island Resort

MAP V2 ▪ Saadiyat Island ▪ 02 498 8888 ▪ www.stregissaadiyatisland.com ▪ DD

A sprawling modern resort situated on a long, idyllic stretch of Saadiyat Island beach. The monumental mock-Tuscan design is a little overwhelming, but the lush grounds create an enjoyably rustic atmosphere, while facilities include several excellent restaurants and a stunning swimming pool.

W Abu Dhabi – Yas Island

MAP W4 ▪ Yas Island ▪ 02 656 0000 ▪ www.marriot.com ▪ DD

Upmarket (but often surprisingly affordable) hotel at the heart of the swanky Yas Marina development. Built directly over the F1 Grand Prix circuit and wrapped in a spectacular illuminated canopy roof, the hotel is one of the city's most memorable modern buildings. Inside, everything is the height of contemporary cool, from the immaculate rooms to a string of very chic restaurants and bars.

Emirates Palace

MAP N1 ■ The Corniche
West ■ 02 690 9000
■ www.emiratespalace.
com ■ DDD

Choose from amongst the
Coral, Pearl and Diamond
Rooms, Khaleej Suites
or Palace Suites at Abu
Dhabi's grandest hotel.
All rooms feature wide
plasma TVs and extras
such as welcome cocktails,
flowers and fruit in the
room, plus butler service.

Inexpensive and Moderate Hotels in Dubai

Ahmedia Heritage Guesthouse

MAP K1 ■ Near Al
Ahmadiya School, Deira
souk ■ 04 225 0085
■ www.heritagedubai
hotels.com ■ D

Book here for a real taste
of heritage flavour. Located
on the Deira side of the
creek, this guesthouse
has spacious, traditionally
styled rooms in a bright
courtyard building.

Arabian Courtyard Hotel & Spa

MAP K2 ■ Al Fahidi St,
opposite Al Fahidi Fort,
Bur Dubai ■ 04 351 9111
■ www.arabiancourtyard.
com ■ D

Views of this historic
area from the Arabian
Courtyard are some of
Dubai's most fascinating.
The Arabian-inspired
rooms are spacious and
the staff friendly.

Barjeel Heritage Guest House

MAP J1 ■ Shindagha,
Bur Dubai ■ 04 354 4424
■ www.heritagedubai
hotels.com ■ D

An attractive heritage
guesthouse in a stunning
setting along the historic
Shindagha waterfront.
The nine rooms are
beautifully decorated in
traditional Arabian style
and there's also a good
little in-house restaurant
serving local-style food.

Golden Sands Hotel Apartments

MAP J2 ■ Al Mankhool St,
Bur Dubai ■ 04 355 5553
■ www.goldensands
dubai.com ■ D

Comfortable self-catering
accommodation in studios
with kitchenettes, close
to supermarkets and
shops in Bur Dubai. All
rooms have a TV and
telephone. Free shuttle
bus to Jumeirah.

Ibis World Trade Centre Hotel

MAP E6 ■ Next to the
Dubai Convention and
Exhibition Centre, Sheikh
Zayed Rd ■ 04 332 4444
■ www.ibishotel.com ■ D

One of Dubai's better
bargains, the Ibis offers
small, clean and stylish
rooms in an excellent
midtown location. The
catch, however, is that
there's no service or extras
for this price, so don't
expect someone to help
with your bags. The hotel
restaurant, Cubo, offers
decent Italian fare.

Orient Guest House

MAP K2 ■ Al Fahidi
Roundabout, Bur Dubai
■ 04 353 4448 ■ www.
heritagedubaihotels.com
■ D

Situated in a renovated
courtyard building in the
historic Al Fahidi neigh-
bourhood, this boutique
hotel is as delightful as
it gets. The traditional
rooms with high ceilings
are decorated in Arabian
and Indian style and
the quiet courtyards are
wonderful for relaxing.

Raintree Hotel

MAP L5 ■ Garhoud Rd,
Deira ■ 04 209 5111
■ www.raintreehotels
dubai.com ■ D

Centrally located behind
Deira city centre, this
smart and competitively
priced modern hotel
offers excellent service,
plus a gym and a rooftop
swimming pool.

XVA

MAP K2 ■ Al Fahidi
■ 04 353 5383 ■ www.
xvahotel.com ■ D

An elegant hotel in a
restored courtyard house,
XVA is full of atmosphere.
The stylish hotel rooms
are minimalist in design.
Don't expect any extras
here; but who needs them
when you can hear the
call-to-prayer echoing
through the streets?

Four Points Sheraton

MAP J2 ■ Khalid Bin
Al-Waleed Rd ■ 04
397 7444 ■ www.four
pointsburdubai.com
■ DD

Convenient for Bur Dubai
souks, Al Fahidi Fort,
the Al Fahidi neighbour-
hood and Burjuman Mall
shopping, this standard
hotel is popular with
business travellers and
tourists on stopovers.

Jumeirah Creekside Hotel

MAP E2 ■ Garhoud
■ 04 230 8555 ■ www.
jumeirah.com ■ DD

Furnished with modern
art and contemporary
designs, this wonderful
hotel offers top-notch
facilities and gorgeous
views of the creek.

For a key to hotel price categories see p112

Inexpensive and Moderate Hotels in Abu Dhabi

Al Ain Palace Hotel
MAP S2 ▪ Corniche Rd East ▪ 02 679 4777 ▪ www.alainpalace hotel.com ▪ D

One of the oldest hotels in the city, it may look its age but still enjoys large, comfortable rooms, a friendly atmosphere and competitive prices. It also has a surprisingly extensive selection of places to eat and drink, making it an attractive option for those who don't feel like heading out after a hot day's sightseeing.

Andaz Capital Gate
MAP U3 ▪ Capital Gate ▪ 02 596 1234 ▪ www.hyatt.com ▪ D

This very smart but also competitively priced hotel is located in the famously leaning Capital Gate tower (see p99). It has cool modern rooms and amazing views from its higher floors. There's also a great spa and a stunning pool.

Hilton Abu Dhabi
MAP N2 ▪ Corniche Rd West ▪ 02 681 1900 ▪ www.hilton.com ▪ D

The Hilton's excellent restaurants and bars have made this hotel a favourite of expats in Abu Dhabi. The hotel has beautiful swimming pools and a Corniche-front beach, lined with shady palm trees. It also offers an array of water sports. Accommodation choices include a variety of spacious and comfortable rooms that come with many little extras – some even offer Gulf views.

Le Royal Meridien
MAP T2 ▪ Khalifa St ▪ 02 674 2020 ▪ www.lemeridien.com ▪ D

All the beautifully appointed rooms at this contemporary hotel have sublime views of both the Corniche and the Arabian Sea, and there are a couple of nice pools concealed amongst the peaceful walled gardens.

Mercure Abu Dhabi Centre
MAP R2 ▪ Hamdan St ▪ 02 633 3555 ▪ www.mercure.com ▪ D

Centrally located, this old hotel looks worn around the edges but is a good choice thanks to its rock-bottom rates and brilliantly central location. Good street views from higher floors.

Millennium Hotel
MAP S1 ▪ Khalifa St ▪ 02 614 6000 ▪ www.millenniumhotels.com ▪ D

A swanky but very reasonably priced hotel. It has elegant and expansive rooms with splendid views over the Corniche, Lulu Island and out to sea. Ideally positioned for Downtown sight-seeing, there is also a small swimming pool.

Sheraton Abu Dhabi Resort & Towers
MAP T1 ▪ Corniche Rd East, Tourist Club area ▪ 02 677 3333 ▪ www.sheraton.com/abudhabi ▪ D

Set right on the Corniche, there are good water and leisure activities at this resort hotel, and its beach-side sheesha spot is truly lovely. Eat at the excellent restaurants on site.

Southern Sun
MAP T1 ▪ Al Mina St ▪ 02 818 4888 ▪ www.tsogosun.com/southern-sun-abu-dhabi ▪ D

Located in central Downtown, this smart but affordable modern hotel has a gym and rooftop pool, plus a couple of top-class restaurants.

Traders Hotel Quaryat al Beri
MAP V4 ▪ Khor al Maqta ▪ 02 510 8888 ▪ www.shangri-la.com/abu dhabi/traders ▪ D

Overlooking Maqta Creek, this above-average mid-range hotel (part of the Shangri-La hotel group) has very smooth service and, for the price, a surprising amount of style. Modern rooms and public areas are decorated with colourful minimalist decor, and there's also a small pool plus private beach.

Beach Rotana
MAP T2 ▪ 10th St, Al Zahiyah ▪ 02 697 9000 ▪ www.rotana.com/beachrotana ▪ DD

A vast resort-style hotel in the heart of Downtown, with smart rooms, a small stretch of beach, private beach club and spa, stunning Al Maryah Island views. It also houses one of the city's best places to eat and drink – the Finz restaurant (see p93) which offers great seafood.

Beyond the Cities

Fujairah Rotana Resort and Spa
E99 coastal highway, Fujairah ▪ 09 244 9888 ▪ www.rotana.com ▪ D

On beautiful Al Aqah Beach, this luxury east

coast resort offers a blissful beachside break from the big cities, with upmarket style and facilities for well under the price of similar hotels in either Dubai or Abu Dhabi. It lies close to the equally large, though less overpowering, Le Méridien Al Aqah.

Al Ain Rotana

120th St, Al Ain ■ 03 754 5111 ■ www.rotana.com/alainrotana ■ DD
The best hotel in Al Ain, centrally located and with a fine array of five-star facilities. The lovely gardens and pools are great for daytime lazing, while the hotel's excellent restaurants, including the Arabian-style Min Zaman and the lively Trader Vics, are enjoyable places to relax after dark.

Anantara Qasr Al Sarab

200 km/120 miles from Abu Dhabi ■ 02 886 2088 ■ www.qasralsarab.anantara.com ■ DD
Looking like something out of Lawrence of Arabia, this magical fortress-style resort sits majestically in the middle of the desert surrounding the spectacular Liwa Oasis, the UAE's finest area of unspoilt wilderness. Rooms feature five-star luxuries and there are private villas, each with a pool and butler service.

Kempinski Hotel Ajman

Ajman ■ 06 714 5555 ■ www.kempinski.com ■ DD
In the tiny emirate of Ajman, just north of Sharjah, the Kempinski offers a convenient

retreat from the big-city bustle of nearby Dubai. Despite this beachfront resort's dated appearance, the hotel remains profoundly relaxing, with fine gardens, a beautiful pool and a private white-sand beach perfect for idle lounging.

Le Méridien Al Aqah Beach Resort

E99 coastal highway, Fujairah ■ 09 244 9000 ■ www.lemeridien-alaqah.com ■ DD
On idyllic Al Aqah Beach with the Hajar Mountains forming the backdrop, this towering resort is one of the east coast's major landmarks, with five-star facilities and huge grounds. It's a good place to set up diving trips.

Melia Desert Palm

Al Awir Rd, Al Ain highway ■ 04 323 8888 ■ www.desertpalm.ae ■ DD
On the fringes of Dubai, around a 20-minute drive from the airport, the intimate Melia Desert Palm resort offers an idyllic retreat from the hectic pace of urban life. The superbly equipped rooms come with private pool and all mod-cons, while the surrounding polo fields create an enjoyably country atmosphere, and the luxurious spa is second to none.

Al Maha Desert Resort and Spa

Dubai Desert Conservation Reserve (60 km/37 miles from Dubai) ■ 04 832 9900 ■ www.al-maha.com ■ DDD
Idyllic desert retreat in the heart of the Dubai Desert Conservation

Reserve. Rare wildlife roams the grounds, almost giving the whole place a feel of an African bush camp, while the lavishly appointed tented suites offer plenty of luxury, including private plunge pools.

Anantara Sir Bani Yas Islands Resort

Sir Bani Yas Island (a 90-minute drive from Abu Dhabi) ■ 02 656 1399 ■ www.sir-bani-yas-island.anantara.com ■ DDD
One of the UAE's most magical – and unusual – places to stay. The resort is located on Sir Bani Yas Island, transformed by Sheikh Zayed in the 1970s into a remarkable nature reserve teeming with wildlife ranging from indigenous Arabian oryx to prancing giraffes. The main resort itself is one of the country's most palatial, and there are also two separate luxury eco-lodges – Al Yamm and Al Sahel – deeper inside the reserve.

Bab Al Shams Desert Resort and Spa

Emirates Rd ■ 04 809 6498 ■ www.meydanhotels.com/babalshams ■ DDD
Spectacular resort hidden away in the desert, just a 45-minute drive from Dubai. Built in the style of a traditional Arabian fort, the resort has top-class facilities including a stunning infinity pool and the memorable Al Hadheerah open-air desert restaurant. This is a great place to enjoy desert activities, such as camel riding and falcony displays.

General Index

Acknowledgments

This edition updated by

Contributor Sarah Hedley Hymers

Senior Editor Alison McGill

Senior Art Editor Stuti Tiwari

Project Editors Alex Pathe, Dipika Dasgupta

Editor Mark Silas

Picture Research Manager Taiyaba Khatoon

Picture Research Administrator Vagisha Pushp

Publishing Assistant Halima Mohammed

Jacket Designer Jordan Lambley

Cartographer Ashif

Cartography Manager Suresh Kumar

Senior DTP Designer Tanveer Zaidi

Senior Production Editor Jason Little

Senior Production Controller Samantha Cross

Deputy Managing Editor Beverly Smart

Managing Editors Shikha Kulkarni, Hollie Teague

Managing Art Editor Sarah Snelling

Senior Managing Art Editor Priyanka Thakur

Art Director Maxine Pedliham

Publishing Director Georgina Dee

DK would like to thank the following for their contribution to the previous editions: Gavin Thomas, Lara Dunston, Sarah Monaghan

The publisher would like to thank the following for their kind permission to reproduce their photographs:

Key: a-above; b-below/bottom; c-centre; f-far; l-left; r-right; t-top

123RF.com: bloodua 45cl; Luciano Mortula 93cl; pio3 73cla; Fedor Selivanov 92b; Oleg Zhukov 26clb.

Alamy Stock Photo: age fotostock 14cla; arabianEye FZ LLC 13tr; Asia Photopress 27tl; AVI Pictures 29tl; Chronicle 36clb; Tibor Bognar 61cl; Yvette Cardozo 14br; China Span / Keren Su 2tr, 34-35b; Dallet-Alba 64cla; eye35.pix 84b; Stuart Forster 98clb; Godong 21tl; Hemis 49br; Hemis.fr / Patrice Hauser 62br; imageBROKER 59tl; John Kellerman 4crb; Feroz Khan 11br; LH Images 10ca, 18bl; Nino Marcutti 7cr, 42b; Iain Masterton 48cl; 71br, 85cla, 91br; Middle East 16cla; Lewis Oliver 10clb; Robertharding 96tl, ; Urbanmyth 98t; WorldTravel 65tr.

Armani Hotel: 12clb.

Asha's: 69br.

Atlantis The Palm – Aquaventure: 44t.

Atlantis, The Palm: 41b, 84tl.

AWL Images: Peter Adams 2tl, 8-9; Walter Bibikow 65b; Alan Copson 49cb; Danita Delimont Stock 15bc; Norbert Eisele-Hein 4cl; Nick Ledger 4b.

Balloon Adventures Dubai: 32-33c.

Burj Al Arab: 4cra, 11tr, 24cr, 25tl, 25cra; Skyview Bar 46t.

Coffee Museum: 18-9, 52bl.

Dreamstime.com: Aleksandra Tokarz 66b; Altayebamer 51tr; Cristian Andriana 54-5, 55t; Badahos 11cr; Beijing Hetuchuangyi Images Co. Ltd. 22-3; Carabiner 79cla; Elnur 28cl; Frantic00 83b; Gmv 45cl; Hayk Harutyunyan 3tr, 102-3; Laszlo Halasi 13bl; Ilonawellington 20-1; Joyshuai 77br; Patryk Kosmider 30-1, 52t, 97tr; Lexandr Lexandrovich 32clb; Lika66 53tr; Manowar1973, 51cl; Miramcor 72b; Luciano Mortula 10tr, 28-9; Manoj Mundapat 54c; Outcast85 94cla; Pazemin 37cl; Photobac 88-9; Pivart 7tl; Romrodinka 76cl; Eq Roy 58cla; Seqoya 24-5; Konstantin Stepanenko 4cla; Petr Švec 28br, 82ca; Swisshippo 14-5,15tr, 30bl; TasFoto 17bl, 50tl; Tea 71tl; Topdeq 10cl; Typhoonski 90cl, 99bl; Thor Jorgen Udvang 42c; Shao Weiwei 11clb; Oleg Zhukov 11cla, 33crb, 60bl.

Dubai Creek Golf & Yacht Club: 16-7, 60t.

The Dubai Mall: 6br

Emaar: 12-13ca

Emirates Palace Abu Dhabi: Sayad 95cra.

Emirates Tower: 70cl.

Getty Images: Jon Arnold 66tr; Allan Baxter 91t; Bloomberg / Christopher Pike 40br; Mark Daffey 78tl; Oliver Furrer 42tl; Matilde Gattoni 49tl; John Harper 78b; Kami Kami 92cla; AFP / Karim Sahib 20clb; Dan Kitwood 44bl; Sebastiaan Kroes 94br; Jean-Pierre Lescourret 68t; Maremagnum 26-7; Iain Masterton 72tl; Moment / Umar Shariff Photography 1; Tuul and Bruno Morandi 10br; Francois Nel 43tr; Frans Sellies 53clb; Sylvain Sonnet 17tl, 18ca; David Steele 59br; Rudy Sulgan 27br; Jochen Tack 31tr; ullstein bild 77t.

Getty Images / iStock: Asia-Pacific Images Studio 4t; celosbyabrar 83tl; Dblight 37br; Chandra Dhas 55crb; Shao Weiwei 31bl; Userc62c9d2b_968 3tl, 56-7.

Jumeirah Zabeel Saray: 40clb.

JW Marriott Marquis Hotel Dubai: Vault 74c.

Karma Kafé: 75bl.

Madinat Jumeirah: Bahri Bar 47clb, 81cra; Shimmers 47tr.

Omega Dubai Desert Classic: 43cl

One&Only Royal Mirage: 41tl, 48b; 86bl; The Rooftop 46clb; Tagine 87cla.

Phocal Media: 21crb, 29crb.

Platinum Heritage: 33tl

Qasr Al Sarab Desert Resort by Anantara: 33bl.

Radisson Blu Hotel / The China Club: 63cla.

Robert Harding Picture Library: Michael DeFreitas 50b.

Souk Madinat Jumeirah: 80b.

Tabari Artspace: 39t.

The Third Line: 38cla.

Towers Rotana Dubai: Long's Bar 74tr.

XVA Gallery, Café & Hotel: 19br; Nathan Root 39br.

Y Bar: 100t.

Yas Abu Dhabi: Atayeb 101br.

Cover

Front and spine: **Getty Images:** Moment / Umar Shariff Photography.

Back: **Alamy Stock Photo:** Iain Masterton tl; **Getty Images:** Moment / Umar Shariff Photography b; **Getty Images / iStock:** adrian825 crb, kertu_ee cla, majaiva tr.

Pull Out Map Cover

Getty Images: Moment / Umar Shariff Photography.

All other images © Dorling Kindersley
For further information see:
www.dkimages.com

Penguin
Random
House

First edition 2007

Published in Great Britain by
Dorling Kindersley Limited
DK, One Embassy Gardens, 8 Viaduct
Gardens, London SW11 7BW, UK

The authorised representative in the EEA is
Dorling Kindersley Verlag GmbH. Arnulfstr.
124, 80636 Munich, Germany

Published in the United States by
DK Publishing, 1745 Broadway, 20th Floor,
New York, NY 10019, USA

Copyright © 2007, 2023 Dorling
Kindersley Limited
A Penguin Random House Company

23 24 25 26 10 9 8 7 6 5 4 3 2 1

The publishers cannot accept responsibility
for any consequences arising from the use
of this book, nor for any material on third
party websites, and cannot guarantee that
any website address in this book will be a
suitable source of travel information.

A CIP catalogue record is available
from the British Library.

A catalogue record for this book is available
from the Library of Congress.

ISSN 1479-344X
ISBN 978-0-2416-2233-9

Printed and bound in Malaysia

www.dk.com

As a guide to abbreviations in visitor information blocks: **Adm** = *admission charge;* **D** = *dinner.*

MIX
Paper | Supporting
responsible forestry
FSC™ C018179

This book was made with Forest
Stewardship Council™ certified
paper – one small step in DK's
commitment to a sustainable future.
**For more information go to
www.dk.com/our-green-pledge**

Phrase Book

In an Emergency

Help!	*Enjedooni*
Stop	*Wak-kaf*
Can you	*Momkin tatlob*
call a doctor?	*tabeeb?*
Can you call an	*Momkin tatlob*
ambulance?	*el es'aaf?*
Can you call the	*Momkin tatlob*
police?	*el shorta?*
Can you call the	*Momkin tatlob*
fire brigade?	*el etfaa?*
Where is the	*Wayn agrab*
nearest hospital?	*mostashfa?*
Is there a telephone here?	*Ako telefoon huna?*

Useful Words and Phrases

Yes	*Na-am*
No	*Laa*
Hello	*Salaam alaikum*
Goodbye	*Ma'aa al salaama*
See you later	*Ela al lekaa*
Excuse me	*'Afwan*
Sorry (said by man)	*Aasif*
Sorry (said by woman)	*Aasifa*
Thank you	*Shakereen*
Please	*Luw tasma`h*
Peace be upon you	*Al salaam 'alaikum*
Peace be upon you (as response)	*Alaikum al salaam*
Good morning	*Sabaa`h al khayr*
Good evening	*Masaa-o al khayr*
Good night	*Tosbihoona ala khayr*
Pleased to meet you	*Ya ahleen*
How are you?	*Keef al 'haal?*
I'm fine	*Zeen*
I don't understand	*Ma afham*
What did he say?	*Shenu kaal?*
Do you speak English?	*Ta'hki enkleezi?*
Does anyone speak English?	*Aku 'hada ye'hkee enkleezi?*
Have you got a table for…?	*Aku taawila hug…?*
I would like to reserve a table	*Areed a'hjiz taawila*
Can I have the bill please?	*Al 'hesaab luw tasma'h*
I am vegetarian	*Ana nabaati*
God willing	*Inshaal-la*
No problem	*Maafi moshkila*
big	*kabeer*
small	*sageer*
hot	*'haar*
cold	*baarid*
bad	*say-ye'e*
good	*tay-yeb*
open	*maftoo'h*
closed	*mesak-kar*
on the right	*'ala al yameen*
on the left	*'ala al yasaar*
near	*kareeb*
far	*ba'eed*
men's toilet	*twalet hug al rejaal*
ladies' toilet	*twalet hug al 'hareem*
a little	*kaleel*
a lot	*waajed*

Making a Telephone Call

Hello	*Aloo*
I'd like to speak to…	*Areed akal-lim…*
This is…	*Ana…*

I'll call back later	*Raa'h at-tasel ba'adeen*
Please say … called	*Khab-birho an-na… et-tasa*

In a Hotel

hotel	*fondok*
Do you have a room?	*Ladaykom 'hojra*
I have a reservation	*Endi 'hajz*
With bathroom	*Bee 'ham-maam*
single room	*'hojra fardiy-ya*
double room	*'hojra le etneen*
porter	*natoor*
shower	*dosh*
key	*meftaa'h*

Sightseeing

art gallery	*ma'arad luw'haal faney-ya*
beach	*shaate'e*
bus station	*muwgaf el baah:*
district	*mentakaa*
entrance	*madkhal*
exit	*makhraj*
garden	*'hadeeka*
guide	*morshid*
guided tour	*morshid al juwla*
map	*khaarta*
mosque	*jaame'a*
museum	*mut'haf*
park	*motanaz-zah*
river	*naher*
taxi	*taksi*
ticket	*tathkara*
tourist office	*maktab seyaa'hi*
Please put the (taxi) meter on	*Luw tasma'h, daw-war al 'ad-daad*
How much is it to…?	*Kam raah tekal-lafni ela…?*
Please take me to (this address)	*Khothni ela (haaza al 'onwaan)*

Shopping

How much is it?	*Kam floos?*
I'd like…	*Areed*
This one	*Haaza*
Do you accept credit cards?	*Hal takbaloon kredit kaard?*
That's too much	*Haaza waayed*
I'll give you…	*Ana raa'h a'ateek…*
I'll take it	*Raa'h aakhdoh*
market	*sook*
expensive	*ghaali*
cheap	*rakhees*
chemist's	*saydalaani*

Menu Decoder

'aish	rice
'aseer	fruit juice
bedoon	without
bee	with
beera	beer
beez	egg
beez maslook	hard-boiled egg
beriaani al dajaaj	chicken biryani
beriaani al lahem	meat biryani
beriaani al robiaan	shrimp biryani
beriaani samak	fish biryani (with bones) spiced tilapia (fish) grilled and served whole
bolti	
da-en	mutton
dajaaj	chicken

faakiha	fruit
falaafel	vegetarian burger made with chickpeas
fee al forn	roasted
fulful	white pepper
fulful aswad	black pepper
gabgab	steamed crab
guhwa	bitter Arabic coffee
haleeb	milk
halwa	Turkish delight with cardamom
ham-moor	local fish that tastes like snapper
ham-moor magli	deep-fried hammoor
harees	gruel cooked in beef stock
heel	cardamom
holo	sweet
kabaab	kebab
kabsa	dish of rice, meat/chicken, dried lemon and saffron
kabsat dajaaj	dish of rice, chicken, dry lemon and saffron
kabsat lahem	dish of rice, meat, dry lemon and saffron
kereem	cream
khal	vinegar made from molasses
khamr	wine
khoboz	bread
khoboz jabaab	large spiced pancakes with cardamom
khoboz shaami	pita bread
khoboz tost	toast
kofta	grilled meatballs
koozi	lamb
koskos	plain couscous
maglee	fried
malh	salt
marag	spiced meat/chicken stock
marag dajaaj	chicken stock
marag lahem	beef stock
mashroob ghaazi	soft drink
mashwi	grilled
mashwi ala el fa`hm	barbecued over coal
masloog	boiled
mohal-li senaa-ee	sweetener
moham-mas	toasted
nabeez	wine
neskafee	coffee
orz	rice
orz bil zafaraan	rice with saffron
robyaan	large grilled shrimp
shai	tea
shawirma	doner kebab
suk-kar	sugar
sulsa	tomato purée cooked in stock
tahye motawas-sit	medium
tshaaw meen dajaaj	chicken chowmein
tshaaw meen lahem	beef chowmein
tshaaw meen samak	seafood chowmein
tshoop sooy	chop suey
wajba khafeefa	snack
zaatar	thyme
zangabeel	ginger powder
zobod	butter

Numbers

1	*waa'hid*
2	*etneen*
3	*thalaatha*
4	*arba'aa*
5	*khamsa*
6	*sit-ta*
7	*saba'a*
8	*thamaaneya*
9	*tes'aa*
10	*'ashra*
11	*'hedaash*
12	*etnaash*
13	*talat-taash*
14	*arba'-taash*
15	*khamastaash*
16	*sit-taash*
17	*saba'ataash*
18	*tamantaash*
19	*tesa'ataash*
20	*eshreen*
21	*waa'hid wa eshreen*
30	*thalatheen*
40	*arbe'een*
50	*khamseen*
60	*sit-teen*
70	*sab'een*
80	*thamaneen*
90	*tes'een*
100	*me-aa*
1000	*alf*

Time

Today	*el yoom*
yesterday	*el bariha*
tomorrow	*baaker*
morning	*sabaa'h*
afternoon	*zaheera*
evening	*masaa*
night	*lail*
now	*al 'heen*
tonight	*el laila*
minute	*dageega*
hour	*sa'aa*
week	*osboo'a*
month	*shahr*
year	*'aam*

Days of the Week

Monday	*al ethneen*
Tuesday	*al thulathaa*
Wednesday	*al arbe'a*
Thursday	*al khamees*
Friday	*al jomo'aa*
Saturday	*al sabet*
Sunday	*al a'had*

Months

January	*yanaayer*
February	*febraayer*
March	*maaris*
April	*abreel*
May	*maayo*
June	*yonyo*
July	*yolyo*
August	*agostos*
September	*sebtamber*
October	*oktoobar*
November	*noovambir*
December	*deesambir*

Dubai Selected Street Index

Abu Dhabi Selected Street Index